Ace the Certified Scrum Master Exam:

250 Practice Questions

1st Edition

www.versatileread.com

Copyright © 2024 VERSAtile Reads. All rights reserved.
This material is protected by copyright, any infringement will be dealt with legal and punitive action.

Document Control

Proposal Name	:	Ace the Certified Scrum Master Exam: 250 Practice Questions
Document Edition	:	1st
Document Release Date	:	28th May 2024
Reference	:	CSM
VR Product Code	:	20241602CSM

Copyright © 2024 VERSAtile Reads.
Registered in England and Wales
www.versatileread.com

All rights reserved. No part of this book may be reproduced or transmitted in any form or by any means, electronic or mechanical, including photocopying, recording, or by any information storage and retrieval system, without the written permission from VERSAtile Reads, except for the inclusion of brief quotations in a review.

Feedback:

If you have any comments regarding the quality of this book or otherwise alter it to better suit your needs, you can contact us through email at info@versatileread.com

Please make sure to include the book's title and ISBN in your message.

About the Contributors:

Nouman Ahmed Khan

AWS/Azure/GCP-Architect, CCDE, CCIEx5 (R&S, SP, Security, DC, Wireless), CISSP, CISA, CISM, CRISC, ISO27K-LA is a Solution Architect working with a global telecommunication provider. He works with enterprises, mega-projects, and service providers to help them select the best-fit technology solutions. He also works as a consultant to understand customer business processes and helps select an appropriate technology strategy to support business goals. He has more than eighteen years of experience working with global clients. One of his notable experiences was his tenure with a large managed security services provider, where he was responsible for managing the complete MSSP product portfolio. With his extensive knowledge and expertise in various areas of technology, including cloud computing, network infrastructure, security, and risk management, Nouman has become a trusted advisor for his clients.

Abubakar Saeed

Abubakar Saeed is a trailblazer in the realm of technology and innovation. With a rich professional journey spanning over twenty-nine years, Abubakar has seamlessly blended his expertise in engineering with his passion for transformative leadership. Starting humbly at the grassroots level, he has significantly contributed to pioneering the Internet in Pakistan and beyond. Abubakar's multifaceted experience encompasses managing, consulting, designing, and implementing projects, showcasing his versatility as a leader.

His exceptional skills shine in leading businesses, where he champions innovation and transformation. Abubakar stands as a testament to the power of visionary leadership, heading operations, solutions design, and integration. His emphasis on adhering to project timelines and exceeding customer expectations has set him apart as a great leader. With an unwavering commitment to adopting technology for operational simplicity and enhanced efficiency, Abubakar Saeed continues to inspire and drive change in the industry.

Dr. Fahad Abdali

Dr. Fahad Abdali is an esteemed leader with an outstanding twenty-year track record in managing diverse businesses. With a stellar educational background, including a bachelor's degree from the prestigious NED University of Engineers & Technology and a Ph.D. from the University of Karachi, Dr. Abdali epitomizes academic excellence and continuous professional growth.

Dr. Abdali's leadership journey is marked by his unwavering commitment to innovation and his astute understanding of industry dynamics. His ability to navigate intricate challenges has driven growth and nurtured organizational triumph. Driven by a passion for excellence, he stands as a beacon of inspiration within the business realm. With his remarkable leadership skills, Dr. Fahad Abdali continues to steer businesses toward unprecedented success, making him a true embodiment of a great leader.

Afreen Iqbal

Afreen Iqbal is a talented and passionate content developer who breathes life into words. With an extensive background in content development, Afreen has honed her skills over the years, transforming ordinary words into immersive literary experiences.

Armed with a profound love for literature and a deep understanding of diverse genres, Afreen curates engaging content that resonates with readers across the globe. Her unique ability to blend creativity with insightfulness allows her to transport audiences into different worlds, each meticulously crafted through her words.

As a content developer, she continues to weave narratives that captivate, educate, and entertain. Her dedication to the craft and her passion make her an ideal guide on the path to leadership excellence, promising readers a delightful and enriching experience.

Table of Contents

Scrum at a Glance 4
    Introduction 4
    Inspect & Adapt: 4
    Agile Development and Scrum: 5
    Scrum's Impact 5
    What is a Professional Scrum Master? 6
    CSM Certification 7
    What to Expect in a CSM Course? 8
    Who Should Take the CSM Course? 8
    CSM Certification Requirements 9
    CSM Certification Costs 9
    CSM Certification Exam 10
    CSM Certification Renewal 10
    Are Scrum Master Certifications Worth It? 10
    CSM Certification Salaries and Jobs 11
Practice Questions 12
Answers 64
About Our Products 120

Scrum at a Glance

Introduction

Scrum is a systematic, step-by-step framework utilized for project and product or application development. It organizes development into concise periods of activity known as Sprints. These Sprints typically span less than one month, often measured in weeks, and occur successively. Each Sprint adheres to a fixed duration, concluding on a predetermined date regardless of whether the work is finished, hence termed as time-boxed.

At the onset of each Sprint, a versatile team comprising various skill sets selects items, typically customer requirements, from a prioritized list. They commit to fulfilling these items by the Sprint's conclusion. Throughout the Sprint, the selected items remain unchanged. Daily, the team convenes briefly to recalibrate its approach, enhancing the likelihood of fulfilling commitments.

As the Sprint draws to a close, the team conducts a comprehensive review with stakeholders, showcasing the progress made and soliciting feedback. This feedback loop informs subsequent Sprints, allowing for continuous improvement and adaptation.

Inspect & Adapt:

Scrum prioritizes the delivery of a truly "done" product by the end of each Sprint. For software, this entails code that is:

- Integrated
- Thoroughly Tested
- Potentially Shippable

A fundamental principle of Scrum is its mantra of "inspect and adapt." Recognizing that development is inherently iterative and involves learning, innovation, and unforeseen challenges, Scrum advocates for a continuous cycle of development. This involves taking incremental steps in development, scrutinizing both the resultant product and the effectiveness of current practices, and subsequently adjusting product goals and process methodologies accordingly. This cyclical process of refinement is integral to the ethos of Scrum, ensuring perpetual evolution and improvement.

Agile Development and Scrum:

Scrum, as you may know by now, is categorized within the agile methodology. The agile framework emerged from traditional iterative and incremental life cycle approaches, rooted in the belief that an approach attuned to human reality and the dynamic nature of product development—marked by learning, innovation, and change—would yield superior outcomes.

The core of agile principles is the emphasis on promptly delivering functional software for hands-on evaluation, as opposed to extensive upfront specification writing. Agile development emphasizes the formation of cross-functional teams empowered to make decisions, rejecting rigid hierarchies and functional compartmentalization. Additionally, it underscores rapid iteration, with ongoing customer involvement throughout the process. Often, when individuals encounter agile development or Scrum, there's a sense of familiarity reminiscent of the early days of start-ups, characterized by a pragmatic "just do it" ethos.

Scrum drew significant inspiration from a seminal 1986 Harvard Business Review article by Professors Takeuchi and Nonaka, which outlined practices associated with successful product development groups. In this article, the term "Scrum" was introduced, drawing parallels between effective development and the coordinated movement of a self-organizing team in rugby. The inaugural Scrum team was established at the Easel Corporation in 1993 by Dr. Jeff Sutherland (the author of this manual), and the Scrum framework was formalized in 1995 through collaboration between Jeff and Ken Schwaber.

Scrum's Impact

Today, Scrum finds application across a spectrum of companies, spanning from industry giants to smaller enterprises, including:

- Technology behemoths such as Google, Yahoo!, Microsoft, and Adobe
- Aerospace and defense leaders like Lockheed Martin, Boeing, and Raytheon
- Prominent research institutions, including Johns Hopkins APL and Los Alamos Laboratories
- Leading software providers such as Siemens, SAP, Oracle, IBM, and Pegasystems
- Telecommunications giants like Nokia, Motorola, British Telecom, and Telefonica/O2
- Networking equipment manufacturers, including Cisco, Alcatel, and Ericsson
- Diverse entities such as GE, Capital One, Wells Fargo, Vanguard, Saxo Bank, and the US Federal Reserve

Teams adopting Scrum methodologies frequently report substantial enhancements and, in certain instances, a complete overhaul in both productivity and team morale. This holds particular significance for product developers who have experienced disillusionment with transient management trends.

What is a Professional Scrum Master?

The Scrum Master within a Scrum team plays a pivotal role in cultivating a conducive and efficient work environment. One of their primary responsibilities involves guiding team members to grasp and embody Scrum values and methodologies. Key attributes commonly associated with a Scrum Master include:

- People-focused mindset
- Exceptional emotional intelligence
- A passion for nurturing personal and professional growth in others

The daily agenda of a Scrum Master often includes facilitating discussions, addressing obstacles hindering the team's progress, and providing guidance to individual team members on Scrum practices. However, the scope of their responsibilities extends far beyond these tasks.

The specific activities and overarching objectives of a Scrum Master may vary depending on the organization. Nonetheless, their core objective remains consistent: enhancing team and organizational agility. As they navigate their role, their focus is directed towards initiatives aimed at fostering continuous improvement and bolstering the team's adaptability.

CSM Certification

Agile practices are swiftly gaining traction in project and product management across diverse industries, underscoring the pivotal role of the ScrumMaster in driving agile development. By enhancing workflow efficiency, the ScrumMaster not only contributes to immediate project success but also augments one's professional value as their career progresses. The Certified ScrumMaster (CSM) certification, administered by the Scrum Alliance, serves as an introductory credential designed to equip professionals with a foundational understanding of Scrum methodologies and values. This includes fostering team performance, fostering accountability, and embracing iterative progress.

Attaining CSM certification offers a multitude of advantages. Firstly, it boosts recognition and credibility as a leader within the agile community. Secondly, it opens up new avenues within organizations that embrace agile practices, providing individuals with enhanced career prospects. Additionally, it furnishes individuals with a competitive edge in future endeavors, serving as a testament to their comprehensive grasp of Scrum principles and practices.

Going beyond the CSM, enrolling in the Advanced Certified ScrumMaster and Certified Scrum Professional® - ScrumMaster courses distinguishes you from the multitude of agile professionals. These certifications validate your advanced expertise and substantial experience as a scrum master, offering compelling talking points during discussions with prospective employers regarding your capacity to bolster agility within their organizations. Opting for the CSP-SM is particularly advantageous if you harbor aspirations of transitioning into roles as a trainer or agile coach.

What to Expect in a CSM Course?

Employers and recruiters highly value the CSM certification, making it one of the most sought-after credentials in the industry. Led by Certified Scrum Trainers® who undergo rigorous evaluation, the certification course covers essential topics outlined in the learning objectives. Trainers may enhance the curriculum with unique examples, exercises, and materials to enrich the learning experience.

Upon course completion, you gain access to the scrum master test. This assessment comprises 50 multiple-choice questions, with a passing score requiring 37 correct answers out of 50. The course fee includes two attempts at the exam.

CSM training equips you with practical skills that you can promptly apply, opening up avenues for career advancement. Upon finishing the course, you'll be fully prepared to take and successfully pass the CSM exam, thereby enhancing your professional credentials.

Who Should Take the CSM Course?

Consider enrolling in the scrum master certification course if any of the following resonate with you:

- You aim to develop a diverse array of professional competencies.
- You seek to enhance your marketability as a prospective employee.
- You are keen on demonstrating to employers and recruiters your dedication to skill enhancement.
- You aspire to gain proficiency in one of the most widely adopted agile frameworks.
- You are intrigued by the notion of embracing an agile mindset rather than adhering strictly to predetermined procedures.
- You aspire to function as a skilled and efficient scrum master.
- You are committed to refining your implementation of scrum principles.
- You are eager to deepen your understanding of agility.

Scrum's application has transcended its origins in software development. Professionals spanning various industries, including marketers, data scientists, HR personnel, and others, are embracing scrum as they seek more effective approaches to product and service development, ultimately aiming to maximize value for customers.

CSM Certification Requirements

Enrolling in CSM training does not require any prerequisites, but completion of the training is necessary to obtain certification. To earn the CSM credential, candidates must possess a solid understanding of the Scrum framework, including its principles and practices.

Candidates are required to attend a CSM course, which typically spans two days in person or four days online and is conducted by a Certified Scrum Trainer. This course offers a comprehensive overview of organizing and supporting a Scrum team, covering essential learning objectives such as scope, Lean, agile methodologies, coaching techniques, and service to the development team, product owner, and organization.

Upon completing the course, candidates are provided with two exam attempts within a 90-day period at no additional cost, facilitated through the Scrum Alliance portal, to achieve Certified ScrumMaster status. However, if additional attempts are needed beyond the initial two, there is a $25 fee per attempt. After successfully passing the CSM exam, candidates must submit a license agreement to the Scrum Alliance for acceptance and complete their Scrum Alliance membership profile.

CSM Certification Costs

The Certified Scrum Trainers cover the initial certification fee for each student who completes a Certified ScrumMaster course successfully. Additionally, the training course fees, which vary from $350 to $1,000, include the following benefits:

- Certification for the first two years
- Two opportunities to take the exam (within 90 calendar days of course completion)

- Course materials provided by instructors during class (must be approved by the Scrum Alliance)
- Access to the two-day course, available either online or in person
- Two-year membership to the Scrum Alliance community

CSM Certification Exam

Understanding the structure and requirements of the Certified ScrumMaster (CSM) exam is crucial for individuals seeking certification in Scrum practices. The CSM exam serves as a validation of one's comprehension of essential Scrum elements. Here's an overview of the exam's format:

- 50 multiple-choice and true/false questions
- 60-minute time limit
- Passing requires 37 correct answers (74%)
- Tests general Scrum knowledge, roles, meetings, and artifacts
- Two free attempts within 90 days of course completion
- $25 fee for additional attempts

CSM Certification Renewal

To maintain your CSM certification, renewal is necessary every two years. This process entails accumulating Scrum Education Units (SEUs) ranging from 10 to 40 hours, along with paying a renewal fee, the amount of which varies based on certification and SEU requirements. Keeping abreast of changes in the field involves acquiring SEUs, with each hour of continuing education equating to one SEU. SEUs are categorized into four groups: events, learning, volunteering, and other independent activities.

Are Scrum Master Certifications Worth It?

Investing in becoming a Certified ScrumMaster proves to be valuable in terms of cost, time, and effort, as it grants you access to an esteemed certification and membership upon successful completion of the examination. This credential serves as a coveted asset on your resume, providing a platform to showcase your proficiency and expertise in agile methodologies during job interviews and discussions regarding promotions.

For numerous individuals, obtaining this certification serves as a launching pad, opening doors to various roles and prospects where they can further cultivate their experience as a Scrum Master and enrich their professional profile.

CSM Certification Salaries and Jobs

Obtaining CSM certification can significantly increase your annual income. Salaries for ScrumMasters vary depending on factors like job title and location. Glassdoor reports an average salary of $128,000, with some positions commanding as much as $165,000. Common job titles associated with this certification include Agile Coach, Scrum Trainer, Senior ScrumMaster, Agile Scrum Coach, and Lead ScrumMaster. Whether you aim for advancement or a new role, CSM certification opens doors to higher-level positions, promising a secure and promising future brimming with opportunities.

Product Questions

Practice Questions

1. When applying the Knoster Model for Managing Complex Change, what is the likely outcome if a change initiative is missing a clear vision?
   A) Resistance
   B) Confusion
   C) Frustration
   D) False Start

2. As a Scrum Master, which of the following is not one of the 6 Facilitation Factors to consider?
   A) Be genuine
   B) Be subjective and biased
   C) Create a mindset of continuous learning
   D) Focus and engagement

3. What is a potential development opportunity for a Scrum Master with a total skill assessment score between 25 and 29?
   A) SAFe Advanced Scrum Master (SASM) training
   B) Professional Scrum Master I certification
   C) No further training is necessary
   D) Basic communication skills workshop

4. What role does the Scrum Master play as "the Model"?
   A) Teaching the team to practice Scrum
   B) Initiating changes within the team
   C) Providing necessary resources to the team
   D) Drafting a detailed project plan

Product Questions

5. If a Scrum Master is skilled at facilitating Scrum events without referring to a checklist, how should this be scored in the skill assessment?
   A) 1
   B) 2
   C) 3
   D) 4

6. According to the Skill and Will Matrix, what should a Scrum Master focus on to help a team member with high skill but low will?
   A) Providing additional technical training
   B) Encouraging the team member's autonomy and purpose
   C) Reducing the team member's responsibilities
   D) Increasing the complexity of the team member's tasks

7. What is the primary responsibility of the Scrum Master as "the Change Agent"?
   A) To teach the fundamentals of Scrum
   B) To implement and manage change effectively
   C) To act as a mediator in conflicts
   D) To provide detailed action plans for the team

8. What are the results when a change initiative lacks the necessary skills, according to the Knoster Model?
   A) Anxiety
   B) Frustration
   C) Resistance
   D) False Start

9. What should a Scrum Master do if their team does not regularly conduct product demos to stakeholders?
   A) Strongly Disagree

B) Somewhat Disagree
C) Somewhat Agree
D) Strongly Agree

10. Which of the following is not an outcome of missing resources when managing complex change?
    A) Frustration
    B) Confusion
    C) Resistance
    D) False Start

11. What is the primary tool used in traditional project management for stakeholder management?
    A) Agile Facilitation
    B) Power and Interest Matrix
    C) SAFe Solutions
    D) Lean Portfolio Management

12. Who is typically responsible for stakeholder management in a Scrum team?
    A) Scrum Master
    B) Product Owner
    C) Both A and B
    D) Project Manager

13. What common mistake do Scrum Masters often make regarding stakeholders?
    A) Over-communicating with stakeholders
    B) Ignoring the stakeholders completely
    C) Not investing enough in building rapport with senior management
    D) Focusing too much on stakeholder needs

Product Questions

14. **How many PDUs can you earn by participating in each Cprime web seminar?**
    A) 1 PDU
    B) 2 PDUs
    C) 5 PDUs
    D) 10 PDUs

15. **Which certification does Mr. Eugene Lai NOT hold?**
    A) Certified Scrum Master (CSM/PSM)
    B) SAFe Solutions Consultant (SSC)
    C) Scaled Agile Program Consultant (SPC)
    D) Agile Certified Practitioner (PMI-ACP)

16. **What is the focus of Lean Portfolio Management as offered by Cprime?**
    A) Increasing the number of Scrum Masters
    B) Validating alignment to business strategy
    C) Developing hardware solutions
    D) Focusing on traditional Waterfall methodologies

17. **What is the primary objective of the Advanced Certified ScrumMaster (A-CSM) course?**
    A) Teaching basic Scrum principles
    B) Providing an in-depth understanding of the ScrumMaster role
    C) Offering a certification in Lean Portfolio Management
    D) Introducing participants to Agile hardware development

18. **Which of the following is NOT included in Cprime's Agile Solutions?**
    A) SAFe Solutions
    B) Agile Transformation

C) Traditional Waterfall/SDLC
D) Agile for Hardware

19. How many corporate PMOs has Mr. Eugene Lai architected?
    A) 3
    B) 5
    C) 6
    D) 7

20. According to the text, what is needed to transition from an experienced Scrum Master to an Advanced Scrum Master?
    A) A high salary
    B) A project management degree
    C) A high level of commitment and a growth mindset
    D) At least 10 years of Scrum experience

21. What is the goal of the Sprint Retrospective?
    A) To plan the next Sprint
    B) To review the work done in the current Sprint
    C) To inspect the team's practices and make improvements
    D) To demonstrate the product to stakeholders

22. What is the purpose of Product Backlog Grooming?
    A) To assign tasks to the Development Team
    B) To refine and prioritize backlog items
    C) To review the increment with stakeholders
    D) To define the Sprint Goal

23. Scrum is a project management method that:
    A) Is used exclusively for software development
    B) Provides flexibility to handle change requests
    C) Requires all requirements to be gathered upfront
    D) Is based on a rigid process

Product Questions

24. Which of the following is not a responsibility of the Product Owner?
A) Facilitating the Daily Scrum
B) Creating and maintaining the Product Backlog
C) Maximizing the value of the product
D) Prioritizing backlog items

25. The Scrum Master is responsible for:
A) Assigning tasks to the Development Team
B) Prioritizing the Product Backlog
C) Ensuring the Scrum framework is followed
D) Defining the product requirements

26. The Product Backlog is:
A) An ordered list of everything needed in the product
B) A detailed plan for the entire project duration
C) A record of completed work items
D) A chart showing the progress of the Sprint

27. The Sprint in Scrum is:
A) A flexible period where the duration can vary
B) A time-boxed iteration of one month or less
C) An ad-hoc meeting for urgent work
D) A phase for planning and documentation

28. What is an Increment in Scrum?
A) The total amount of work completed in a Sprint
B) A list of tasks for the next Sprint
C) A set of features released to the customer
D) The sum of all Product Backlog items completed during a Sprint and all previous Sprints

Product Questions

29. Which project would benefit from using traditional methods over Scrum?
    A) A project with a well-defined scope and few expected changes
    B) A project where the requirements are unknown and likely to change
    C) A project with an unclear product description upfront
    D) A project where incremental results have value

30. Why is it important for all roles to receive Scrum training before starting a project?
    A) To ensure that the Scrum Master can assign tasks effectively
    B) To make sure all parties understand their roles and responsibilities
    C) To allow the Development Team to work without a Scrum Master
    D) To guarantee that the Product Owner can work alone without a team

31. What is the primary role of the Scrum Master?
    A) To manage the project schedule
    B) To facilitate Scrum events and ensure the framework is followed
    C) To prioritize the Product Backlog
    D) To write user stories for the Product Backlog

32. What is the primary responsibility of the Product Owner in Scrum?
    A) To manage the project budget
    B) To maintain and prioritize the Product Backlog
    C) To assign tasks to the Development Team
    D) To facilitate Daily Scrum meetings

Product Questions

33. What does the Sprint Backlog consist of?
   A) All items from the Product Backlog
   B) Only high-priority items from the Product Backlog
   C) Selected items for the upcoming Sprint
   D) Completed items from the previous Sprint

34. How long is a typical Sprint duration?
   A) 1 week
   B) 2 weeks
   C) 30 days
   D) It varies based on project complexity

35. What is the purpose of the Daily Scrum meeting?
   A) To review the work completed
   B) To provide a status update to the Product Owner
   C) To plan work for the next 24 hours
   D) To retrospect the previous Sprint

36. When can a Sprint Backlog be updated?
   A) Only during the Sprint Planning
   B) Anytime during the Sprint as needed
   C) After the Sprint Review
   D) It cannot be changed once the Sprint starts

37. Who is responsible for creating the Definition of "Done"?
   A) The Scrum Master
   B) The Product Owner
   C) The Development Team
   D) The whole Scrum Team

38. What is an Increment in Scrum?
   A) The total list of product features

B) The sum of all Product Backlog items completed during a Sprint
C) The progress report presented during the Daily Scrum
D) The initial product draft

39. **Who attends the Sprint Planning meeting?**
    A) The Scrum Master only
    B) The Development Team only
    C) The Product Owner only
    D) The whole Scrum Team

40. **At what event is the Sprint Backlog created?**
    A) During the Daily Scrum
    B) At the Sprint Planning meeting
    C) At the Sprint Review
    D) During the Sprint Retrospective

41. **Who is responsible for prioritizing the Product Backlog?**
    A) The Scrum Master
    B) The Product Owner
    C) The Development Team
    D) The stakeholders

42. **What is the primary purpose of the Sprint Review?**
    A) To plan the next Sprint
    B) To demonstrate the work done during the Sprint
    C) To assign tasks for the next Sprint
    D) To update the Product Backlog

43. **What is the goal of the Sprint Retrospective?**
    A) To update the Product Backlog
    B) To demonstrate the Increment to stakeholders

C) To reflect on the past Sprint and identify improvements
D) To celebrate the completion of the Sprint

44. **What is the main characteristic of a Scrum Team?**
    A) It is led by the Scrum Master
    B) It is self-organizing and cross-functional
    C) It consists of stakeholders and users
    D) It reports to the Product Owner

45. **What is the purpose of the Product Backlog Grooming session?**
    A) To assign tasks to developers
    B) To estimate the product features
    C) To refine the Product Backlog items and ensure they are ready for future Sprints
    D) To review the team's performance

46. **How often does the Product Backlog get updated?**
    A) Only at the start of the project
    B) Once every Sprint
    C) Continuously throughout the project
    D) Only when the Product Owner decides

47. **What artifact is used to monitor Sprint's progress?**
    A) The Increment
    B) The Sprint Goal
    C) The Burndown Chart
    D) The Product Roadmap

48. **Who has the authority to cancel a Sprint?**
    A) The Development Team
    B) The Scrum Master

Product Questions

   C) The Product Owner
   D) Any stakeholder

49. **What event marks the start of a new Sprint?**
    A) The Sprint Review
    B) The Daily Scrum
    C) The Sprint Planning Meeting
    D) The Sprint Retrospective

50. **What is a key characteristic of the Product Backlog?**
    A) It is ordered by the Scrum Master
    B) It is a closed list with no changes allowed
    C) It is an ordered list of everything that might be needed in the product
    D) It is fixed for the duration of the project

51. **What is the role of the Scrum Master during the Daily Scrum?**
    A) To report to the Product Owner
    B) To lead the meeting and assign tasks
    C) To ensure the meeting is productive and stays within the time box
    D) To take notes and update the Sprint Backlog

52. **What is the maximum duration for a Sprint?**
    A) 2 weeks
    B) 30 days
    C) 4 weeks
    D) It is not time-boxed

53. **How is work assigned to the Development Team members in Scrum?**
    A) By the Scrum Master

B) By the Product Owner
C) By the Development Team itself
D) By the stakeholders

54. What is the main focus of the Scrum framework?
A) Creating comprehensive documentation
B) Following a predefined project plan
C) Delivering value through iterative progress
D) Finalizing the project within the initial estimates

55. What is a User Story in the context of Scrum?
A) A detailed specification of a software feature
B) A high-level definition of a requirement, focusing on the value it provides to the customer
C) A technical description of a task
D) A report on the progress of a Sprint

56. Which of the following is not a Scrum Artifact?
A) Product Backlog
B) Sprint Backlog
C) Increment
D) Gantt Chart

57. What is the outcome of the Sprint Planning meeting?
A) The Product Roadmap
B) The Sprint Goal and Sprint Backlog
C) The Increment
D) The Definition of "Done"

58. How should the Product Backlog items be sorted?
A) By size of the items
B) By the order of their technical dependencies

Product Questions

C) By the order of importance and value
D) Alphabetically

59. Who can attend the Sprint Review?
A) Only the Scrum Team
B) Only the Development Team and Product Owner
C) The Scrum Team and any interested stakeholders
D) Only the Scrum Master and Product Owner

60. What is the primary purpose of the Sprint Goal?
A) To provide a detailed list of features for the Sprint
B) To define the business purpose and objective of the Sprint
C) To set a strict deadline for the Sprint
D) To allocate specific tasks to Development Team members

61. What is the role of the Product Owner in a Scrum team?
A) To facilitate Scrum events and coach the team
B) To be responsible for the technical aspects of product development
C) To maximize the value of the product and work of the Development Team
D) To remove impediments for the Development Team

62. How many roles are defined in a Scrum project?
A) Two
B) Three
C) Four
D) As many as needed

63. What does the term "Scrum Team" refer to?
A) Only the Development Team
B) The Development Team and Scrum Master

C) The Product Owner and Scrum Master
D) The Product Owner, Scrum Master, and the Development Team

64. Which role in Scrum is considered a 'servant-leader'?
    A) Product Owner
    B) Scrum Master
    C) Development Team member
    D) Project Manager

65. How many people typically make up a Scrum Development Team?
    A) 1-2
    B) 3-9
    C) 10-15
    D) 16-20

66. What is the primary planning tool in Scrum?
    A) Sprint Backlog
    B) Product Backlog
    C) Burndown chart
    D) Increment

67. Can a person have multiple roles in Scrum?
    A) Yes, it is recommended.
    B) Yes, but it is not recommended.
    C) No, it is not allowed.
    D) Only if they are a Scrum Master and Development Team member.

68. What are the two essential characteristics of a Scrum Team?
    A) Self-organized and cross-functional
    B) Cross-functional and hierarchical

C) Self-organized and role-specific
D) Hierarchical and role-specific

69. Who is responsible for removing impediments in a Scrum project?
   A) Product Owner
   B) Scrum Master
   C) Development Team
   D) Project Manager

70. What is the recommended way for Development Team members to work on projects?
   A) Part-time on multiple projects
   B) Full-time on multiple projects
   C) Part-time on a single project
   D) Full-time on a single project

71. Who is accountable for the tasks in the Sprint Backlog?
   A) The individual who performs the task
   B) The Scrum Master
   C) The Product Owner
   D) The entire Development Team

72. Who sets the order of items in the Product Backlog?
   A) Scrum Master
   B) Development Team
   C) Product Owner
   D) External stakeholders

73. True or False: The Product Owner is always someone from the customer's organization.
   A) True
   B) False

Product Questions

74. **What should the composition of a Development Team be like?**
    A) Constantly changing to adapt
    B) Changed only during Sprints
    C) Should not change often
    D) Defined by the Scrum Master

75. **Does Scrum prescribe a role for traditional project managers?**
    A) Yes, as a Scrum Master
    B) Yes, as a Product Owner
    C) No, it distributes their responsibilities
    D) No, it eliminates their role entirely

76. **Is it possible to have a committee for the Product Owner role?**
    A) Yes, and it's common practice
    B) Yes, but there must be a single representative
    C) No, it's not allowed in Scrum
    D) Only if the Scrum Master approves

77. **What is a key responsibility of the Product Owner regarding the Product Backlog?**
    A) To assign tasks to Development Team members
    B) To ensure each item is well understood by stakeholders
    C) To facilitate Daily Scrum meetings
    D) To remove impediments for the team

78. **Which Scrum role is responsible for coaching the Product Owner?**
    A) Development Team member
    B) Scrum Master

Product Questions

C) Project Manager
D) External Consultant

79. True or False: The Development Team should be cross-functional and include roles like designer, tester, and team leader.
   A) True
   B) False
   C) True, but only for large teams
   D) False unless specified by the Product Owner

80. Which Scrum event is used to demonstrate completed work to the customer?
   A) Sprint Planning
   B) Sprint Review
   C) Daily Scrum
   D) Sprint Retrospective

81. What should happen if the Scrum Team composition needs to change?
   A) Change should occur mid-sprint to challenge the team
   B) Change should never happen once the team is formed
   C) Change should occur between Sprints to minimize disruption
   D) The Scrum Master should decide when to change the team

82. Who is responsible for prioritizing the Product Backlog?
   A) The Scrum Master
   B) The Development Team
   C) The Product Owner
   D) The Customer

83. What is an Increment in Scrum?
   A) A task in the Sprint Backlog

B) A potentially releasable part of the final product
C) A measure of a team member's performance
D) A project management tool

84. Who ensures that the Scrum framework is correctly implemented?
    A) Product Owner
    B) Scrum Master
    C) Development Team
    D) Project Manager

85. What is the recommended full-time work status for Scrum Team members?
    A) Full-time status is recommended for maximum focus and productivity
    B) Part-time status is recommended for flexibility
    C) Full-time status is optional based on project size
    D) Part-time status is encouraged to promote work-life balance

86. What does a Burndown chart monitor?
    A) Progress toward a Sprint goal
    B) Product Backlog item prioritization
    C) Increment releases
    D) Stakeholder satisfaction

87. What is the Scrum Master's role regarding impediments?
    A) To assign them to team members
    B) To resolve or remove them
    C) To prioritize them in the Product Backlog
    D) To report them to the customer

88. What is the size range of a Scrum Team, including all three roles?

Product Questions

    A) 4-11
    B) 5-12
    C) 3-11
    D) 6-14

89. Who measures the performance of a Scrum project?
    A) The Development Team
    B) The customer
    C) The Product Owner
    D) The Scrum Master

90. What happens in the Sprint Retrospective?
    A) The team demonstrates the completed work
    B) The team plans the next Sprint
    C) The team discusses improvements for the next Sprint
    D) The team decomposes stories into tasks

91. What is the maximum duration for a Sprint in Scrum?
    A) 2 weeks
    B) 1 month
    C) 6 weeks
    D) Indefinite

92. Who is responsible for maximizing the value of the product Scrum Team?
    A) Scrum Master
    B) Development Team
    C) Product Owner
    D) Project Manager

93. Which of the following is NOT a standard role in Scrum?
    A) Product Owner
    B) Scrum Master

Product Questions

C) Quality Assurance Manager
D) Development Team Member

94. **What is the purpose of the Sprint Planning event?**
    A) To present the completed work to stakeholders
    B) To plan the work for the next Sprint
    C) To review the previous Sprint's work and identify improvements
    D) To monitor daily progress

95. **How long is the Daily Scrum supposed to last?**
    A) 30 minutes
    B) 15 minutes
    C) 1 hour
    D) It varies based on team size

96. **What should the Development Team do if they cannot complete an item by the end of the Sprint?**
    A) Continue working into the next Sprint
    B) Cancel the Sprint
    C) Re-estimate and carry forward to the next Sprint
    D) Present it as partially done in the Sprint Review

97. **Who is responsible for conducting the Sprint Retrospective?**
    A) Product Owner
    B) Scrum Master
    C) Development Team
    D) None of the above

98. **Which of the following best describes the Increment in Scrum?**
    A) The items completed during a single Sprint
    B) The total work completed by the end of the project

C) The sum of all Product Backlog items completed during a Sprint and all previous Sprints
D) The initial project plan

99. Who can cancel a Sprint?
    A) Scrum Master
    B) Development Team
    C) Product Owner
    D) Any stakeholder

100. What is the main reason for time-boxing events in Scrum?
    A) To ensure that the team works overtime
    B) To ensure regularity and minimize complexity
    C) To prevent the Development Team from taking breaks
    D) To allow for unlimited changes to the Sprint Backlog

101. What is the typical duration of a Sprint Review for a one-month Sprint?
    A) 2 hours
    B) 4 hours
    C) 6 hours
    D) 8 hours

102. What is the maximum recommended time for Product Backlog grooming activities during a Sprint?
    A) 5%
    B) 10%
    C) 15%
    D) 20%

103. What is a Burndown Chart used for in Scrum?
    A) To schedule future Sprints

Product Questions

B) To track remaining work in the Sprint
C) To document the Sprint Retrospective outcomes
D) To plan the Sprint Review presentation

104. **What is the Sprint Goal?**
   A) A detailed list of tasks for the Sprint
   B) The estimated velocity of the Development Team
   C) An objective set by the Scrum Master
   D) An objective that will be met within the Sprint through the implementation of the Product backlog

105. **Which event is designed explicitly for process improvement?**
   A) Sprint Planning
   B) Daily Scrum
   C) Sprint Review
   D) Sprint Retrospective

106. **What happens to incomplete Product Backlog items at the end of a Sprint?**
   A) They are discarded
   B) They are automatically rolled into the next Sprint
   C) They are re-estimated and returned to the Product Backlog
   D) They are completed in the slack time

107. **Who facilitates the Daily Scrum meeting?**
   A) Product Owner
   B) Scrum Master
   C) Development Team
   D) External stakeholders

108. **What is the role of the Scrum Master during the Sprint Review?**

Product Questions

A) To present the Increment to stakeholders
B) To facilitate the meeting
C) To prioritize the Product Backlog items
D) To re-estimate the incomplete items

109. When can changes be made to the Sprint Backlog?
A) Anytime during the Sprint
B) Only during the Daily Scrum
C) After the Sprint Review
D) During the next Sprint Planning

110. Who is responsible for ordering the items in the Product Backlog?
A) Scrum Master
B) Development Team
C) Product Owner
D) Customer

111. What does it mean for a Product Backlog item to be "Done"?
A) It is 50% complete
B) It has been started by the Development Team
C) It meets the criteria defined in the "Definition of Done"
D) It has been reviewed by the Product Owner

112. What does the Scrum Master do if the Development Team is blocked by an impediment?
A) Takes over the task
B) Reassigns the task to another team
C) Works to remove the impediment
D) Cancels the Sprint

113. What is the recommended number of people in the Development Team?

A) 1-2
B) 3-9
C) 10-15
D) More than 15

114. **Which of the following best describes the role of the Scrum Master?**
    A) A team leader who assigns tasks
    B) A project manager who controls the project schedule
    C) A coach and facilitator who ensures the Scrum process is followed
    D) A customer representative who prioritizes the work

115. **What should a Scrum Team do if the composition of the Development Team changes?**
    A) Cancel the current Sprint
    B) Continue with the Sprint without any adjustments
    C) Re-plan the Sprint
    D) Avoid changing the composition during a Sprint

116. **What is the main focus of Scrum?**
    A) Following a detailed project plan
    B) Completing as many tasks as possible
    C) Delivering high-quality documentation
    D) Delivering valuable product increments

117. **Who should attend the Sprint Retrospective?**
    A) Only the Development Team
    B) Only the Scrum Master and Product Owner
    C) All members of the Scrum Team
    D) All stakeholders, including customers

118. **What is the primary artifact created during Sprint Planning?**
    A) Sprint Goal
    B) Product Roadmap
    C) Sprint Backlog
    D) Increment

119. **When is the Product Backlog created and maintained?**
    A) Only at the beginning of the project
    B) At the beginning and then during each Sprint Review
    C) Continuously throughout the project
    D) During the Sprint Retrospective

120. **What is the role of the Product Owner during the Daily Scrum?**
    A) To direct the Development Team's work for the day
    B) To participate and provide updates
    C) To ensure the meeting starts on time
    D) The Product Owner does not have a role in the Daily Scrum

121. **What is the main focus of the Agile Manifesto?**
    A) Comprehensive documentation
    B) Contract negotiation
    C) Individuals and interactions
    D) Following a strict plan

122. **Which statement is NOT true about Scrum?**
    A) Developers work within a predefined framework
    B) The Scrum Master is like a traditional project manager
    C) Scrum requires a Business Case
    D) The Product Owner manages the day-to-day activities of the Team

Product Questions

123. **Who is responsible for creating and maintaining the Product Backlog?**
    A) The Scrum Master
    B) The Development Team
    C) The Product Owner
    D) The Project Manager

124. **What is the time limit for a Daily Scrum meeting?**
    A) 15 minutes
    B) 30 minutes
    C) 1 hour
    D) There is no time limit

125. **What is the purpose of 'Slack' in Scrum?**
    A) To allocate extra time for backlog refinement
    B) To provide a buffer for unplanned work
    C) To extend the Sprint duration
    D) To delay the Sprint Review

126. **In Scrum, who takes on the responsibilities similar to a traditional Project Manager?**
    A) The Scrum Master
    B) The Product Owner
    C) The Development Team
    D) There is no equivalent role

127. **Which artifact provides information about the work to be performed in the Sprint?**
    A) Product Backlog
    B) Sprint Backlog
    C) Increment
    D) Definition of Done

Product Questions

128. **What does the Definition of "Done" signify in Scrum?**
   A) The completion of the Sprint
   B) The end of the Daily Scrum
   C) The criteria for accepting work as completed
   D) The final product delivery

129. **Self-assessment is essential in Scrum to:**
   A) Evaluate the Product Owner's performance
   B) Assess the market value of the product
   C) Reflect on the Scrum process and improve it
   D) Determine the project's return on investment

130. **Scrum is more suitable than traditional methods when:**
   A) Requirements change frequently
   B) Scope is clearly defined upfront
   C) Few changes are expected during the project
   D) Users cannot start using the products until the project is complete

131. **What is a time box in the context of Scrum?**
   A) A storage area for project documents
   B) An uninterrupted period for deep work
   C) A maximum duration for a Scrum event
   D) A schedule for releasing the product increments

132. **Which artifact helps in monitoring Sprint's progress?**
   A) Sprint Burndown Chart
   B) Product Backlog
   C) Sprint Backlog
   D) Release Plan

133. **In Scrum, who is responsible for maximizing the value of the product?**

A) The Scrum Master
B) The Development Team
C) The Product Owner
D) The stakeholders

134. **What happens to the traditional project manager role in a Scrum project?**
    A) It is divided between the Product Owner and the Scrum Master
    B) It is taken on by the Development Team
    C) It is completely eliminated
    D) It is replaced by the role of a coach

135. **The' Slack' concept in Scrum is similar to which traditional project management practice?**
    A) Resource leveling
    B) Contingency reserve
    C) Critical path method
    D) Earned value management

136. **Which of the following best describes the nature of Scrum events?**
    A) Optional and informal
    B) Prescribed and time-boxed
    C) Spontaneous and irregular
    D) Long and detailed

137. **The Development Team in Scrum is characterized by:**
    A) Fixed roles for each member
    B) Specialization in one area of work
    C) Cross-functionality and self-organization
    D) Reporting to the Product Owner

Product Questions

138. **Who attends the Sprint Planning meeting?**
   A) The Development Team only
   B) The Scrum Master and Development Team
   C) The Scrum Master, Product Owner, and Development Team
   D) The Product Owner only

139. **How is progress toward a goal monitored in Scrum?**
   A) Through status update meetings
   B) With a comprehensive documentation
   C) Using artifacts like the Sprint Burndown Chart
   D) By the number of completed tasks

140. **Which of the following is an actual fact about Scrum?**
   A) Scrum eliminates all paperwork.
   B) Scrum is difficult, complex, and challenging to implement without proper training.
   C) The Scrum Master decides what will be delivered.
   D) Scrum tells us everything about managing projects.

141. **What is the primary purpose of a Certified ScrumMaster (CSM) course?**
   A) To teach ancillary topics
   B) To provide a prescriptive methodology of Scrum
   C) To cover specific Learning Objectives based on the Scrum Guide and Agile Manifesto
   D) To focus solely on the roles within Scrum

142. **Which of the following is NOT a category of the CSM Learning Objectives?**
   A) Agile Coaching
   B) Scrum Event Planning
   C) Service to the Development Team
   D) Service to the Organization

Product Questions

143. **According to the Learning Objectives, what is Scrum primarily considered to be?**
    A) A methodology
    B) A framework
    C) A process
    D) A tool

144. **Which of the following is NOT a Scrum value?**
    A) Respect
    B) Openness
    C) Efficiency
    D) Focus

145. **What is the maximum recommended size for a Development Team in Scrum?**
    A) Fewer than three people
    B) Three people
    C) Three to nine people
    D) Ten or more people

146. **Why should the Product Owner be a single person and not a group?**
    A) To simplify communication
    B) To have a clear line of authority
    C) To avoid decision-making delays
    D) All of the above

147. **What are the three pillars of empirical process control in Scrum?**
    A) Inspection, Adaptation, Transparency
    B) Planning, Execution, Review

C) Vision, Framework, Practice
D) Requirement, Design, Testing

148. What does the Scrum Master facilitate during the Daily Scrum?
A) The conversation, if necessary
B) The three questions agenda
C) Both A and B
D) Assigning tasks to team members

149. What is the outcome of every Sprint?
A) A prepared product backlog
B) A potentially releasable product increment
C) A fully completed product
D) A report on the team's performance

150. During Sprint Planning, what are one input and two outputs of the event?
A) Input: Completed tasks, Outputs: New tasks, Sprint goal
B) Input: "Ready" product backlog items, Outputs: Sprint goal, Sprint backlog
C) Input: Sprint backlog, Outputs: Product backlog, Release plan
D) Input: Stakeholder feedback, Outputs: Product roadmap, Development strategy

151. Which of the following is NOT a responsibility of the Development Team during Sprint Planning?
A) Provide a forecast
B) Decide how much work is brought into the Sprint
C) Offer the Sprint goal
D) Create Sprint backlog items

Product Questions

152. **What is the role of the Scrum Master in relation to impediments?**
   A) To assign someone to deal with impediments
   B) To make impediments visible and work with the team to resolve them
   C) To ignore impediments as they are the team's responsibility
   D) To solve all impediments themselves

153. **What does time boxing refer to in Scrum?**
   A) Limiting the time spent on product development
   B) Setting fixed durations for project phases
   C) Allocating fixed time periods for Scrum events
   D) Restricting the time allowed for meetings

154. **What is an essential characteristic of the product backlog?**
   A) It is fixed and unchangeable
   B) It is dynamic and ordered
   C) It is maintained solely by the Scrum Master
   D) It contains fully detailed product specifications

155. **Which of the following is NOT an element of a product backlog item?**
   A) Description
   B) Order
   C) Deadline
   D) Estimate

156. **Whose responsibility is it to provide estimates for the product backlog items?**
   A) The Scrum Master
   B) The Product Owner

Product Questions

C) The Development Team
D) The stakeholders

157. **What does the Scrum Master do with the Definition of Done?**
    A. Creates it unilaterally
    B. Facilitates its creation
    C. Ignores it as it is not their responsibility
    D. Enforces it without team input

158. **What is the maximum amount of time the Development Team should spend on product backlog refinement?**
    A) 10% of their capacity
    B) 25% of their capacity
    C) 50% of their capacity
    D) No fixed time; it varies per sprint

159. **What is the impact of a strong Definition of Done?**
    A) It limits the creativity of the Development Team
    B) It reduces the transparency of the Sprint
    C) It ensures a high-quality product increment
    D) It increases the duration of the Sprint

160. **What is NOT a responsibility of the Product Owner during the Sprint Review?**
    A) Explain which product backlog items have been "Done."
    B) Track total work remaining toward a goal
    C) Assign tasks for the next Sprint
    D) Demonstrate the results of the Sprint

161. **What does the term 'technical debt' refer to in Scrum?**
    A) The financial expenses incurred by the team
    B) The incomplete documentation of the product

Product Questions

C) The consequences of poor system design or software architecture
D) The cost of additional features added to the product backlog

162. **In the context of Scrum, what is the main difference between a framework and a methodology?**
    A) A framework is prescriptive, while a methodology is flexible
    B) A framework provides a structure, while a methodology describes precise practices
    C) A framework focuses on software development, while a methodology is for general management
    D) A framework is only for small teams, while a methodology is for larger organizations

163. **What does the Scrum Master do as a Servant-Leader for the team?**
    A) Gives orders to the team
    B) Acts as the team's secretary
    C) Facilitates team processes and supports the team's growth
    D) Manages the product backlog

164. **What is the Sprint Backlog?**
    A) A list of product features requested by the stakeholders
    B) A detailed plan for the entire project
    C) A real-time snapshot of the Development Team's work for the Sprint
    D) A record of completed product backlog items

165. **What happens if the Scrum Team fails to adopt Scrum in its entirety?**
    A) The team becomes more efficient
    B) The Scrum Master takes on more responsibilities

C) Some organizational benefits of Scrum are lost
D) The team is required to restart the project

166. **Why should multiple teams working on the same product have an identical product backlog?**
A) To ensure consistent product quality
B) To create competition between teams
C) To allow teams to work in isolation
D) To make the product backlog shorter

167. **What is the key responsibility of the Product Owner regarding the product backlog?**
A) Writing the code for product backlog items
B) Ensuring a shared understanding of product backlog items
C) Solving technical issues within the product backlog items
D) Time-boxing the development work for product backlog items

168. **What is the negative impact of excessive time pressure applied by the Product Owner on the Development Team?**
A) Increased innovation
B) Higher quality
C) Reduced morale
D) Faster delivery

169. **What is the Sprint Goal?**
A) A detailed list of tasks to be completed during the Sprint
B) The maximum amount of work the Development Team can commit to
C) An objective set during Sprint Planning that provides guidance to the Development Team on why it is building the increment
D) The total hours the Development Team will work in the Sprint

Product Questions

170. **Why are traditional project managers not present in Scrum?**
    A) Because Scrum is only for small projects
    B) Because the role is redundant with the Scrum Master
    C) Because traditional project management activities are distributed among the Scrum roles
    D) Because Scrum does not involve complex projects

171. **What is the relationship between Scrum and the Agile Manifesto?**
    A) Scrum is a subset of the Agile Manifesto principles.
    B) Scrum competes with the Agile Manifesto.
    C) Scrum is a prescriptive methodology derived from the Agile Manifesto.
    D) Scrum is a framework that aligns with the Agile Manifesto principles.

172. **Which of the following best describes empirical process control in Scrum?**
    A) A process where decisions are made based on seniority and experience.
    B) A process that is defined and unchangeable once implemented.
    C) A process that is based on observation, experimentation, and evidence.
    D) A process controlled by a central authority.

173. **What Scrum values should be present in a Scrum event, artifact, or role?**
    A) Efficiency, Predictability, Control, and Hierarchy
    B) Focus, Courage, Commitment, Openness, and Respect

Product Questions

C) Planning, Directing, Reporting, and Budgeting
D) Quality, Speed, Flexibility, and Innovation

174. **Why is Scrum considered a framework rather than a methodology?**
A) Because it provides a set of detailed instructions for managing software development projects.
B) Because it is a rigid structure that cannot be adapted.
C) Because it provides a broad structure under which various processes and techniques can be employed.
D) Because it rejects any principles of the Agile Manifesto.

175. **How many roles are there in a Scrum Team, and what are they?**
A) Two roles: the Scrum Master and the Product Owner.
B) Three roles: the Scrum Master, the Product Owner, and the Development Team.
C) Four roles: the Scrum Master, the Product Owner, the Project Manager, and the Development Team.
D) Five roles: the Scrum Master, the Product Owner, the Development Team, the Stakeholders, and the Users.

176. **Which of the following is NOT a prerogative of the Product Owner?**
A) Defining the scope for the Development Team.
B) Deciding when to release the product.
C) Assigning specific tasks to Development Team members.
D) Maximizing the value of the Scrum Team's product.

177. **What is one of the main reasons why the Product Owner is a single person and not a committee?**
A) To reduce the overall cost of the project.
B) To ensure that there is a clear, singular vision for the product.

Product Questions

C) To simplify the organizational hierarchy.
D) To allow for more features to be requested.

178. **What is the outcome of every sprint?**
   A) A comprehensive report on team performance.
   B) A potentially releasable product increment.
   C) The completion of all product backlog items.
   D) A new set of requirements for the next sprint.

179. **Which of the following is a responsibility of the Scrum Master during sprint planning?**
   A) Deciding how much work is brought into the sprint.
   B) Providing clarification on product backlog items.
   C) Facilitating the dialogue between the team and the Product Owner.
   D) Offering the sprint goal.

180. **What is the definition of technical debt?**
   A) The amount of money spent on technology upgrades.
   B) The total number of unresolved bugs in a product.
   C) The extra development work that arises when code that is easy to implement in the short run is used instead of applying the best overall solution.
   D) The cost of additional features added to a product after its initial release.

181. **What is Scrum?**
   A) A management fad
   B) A fixed-duration project cycle
   C) An iterative, incremental framework for development
   D) A type of software

Product Questions

182. **What is the duration of a Sprint in Scrum?**
   A) More than a month
   B) Variable
   C) Up to a month
   D) Yearly

183. **What happens at the beginning of a Sprint?**
   A) The team takes a break
   B) Stakeholders review the project
   C) A cross-functional team selects items to complete
   D) The project is completed

184. **What does Scrum of a Sprint?**
   A) A detailed report
   B) A set of new requirements
   C) A working product that is "done."
   D) A fully documented design

185. **What is the central theme in Scrum?**
   A) Inspect and adapt
   B) Command and control
   C) Predict and follow
   D) Plan and execute

186. **What type of teams does Agile development focus on?**
   A) Outsourced teams
   B) Cross-functional teams empowered to make decisions
   C) Hierarchical teams
   D) Individual contributors

187. **What is the origin of the term "Scrum"?**
   A) A type of software bug
   B) A military strategy

C) A restart in the game of rugby

D) A business theory

188. **What did the 1986 Harvard Business Review article relate to successful development?**
A) Waterfall methodologies
B) The game of Rugby
C) Traditional project management
D) Financial models

189. **Who are the founders of Scrum?**
A) Bill Gates and Paul Allen
B) Steve Jobs and Steve Wozniak
C) Jeff Sutherland and Ken Schwaber
D) Larry Page and Sergey Brin

190. **What is the purpose of the daily meeting during a Sprint?**
A) To socialize
B) To re-plan work to meet commitments
C) To report to management
D) To extend the Sprint

191. **Scrum is often said to be not a silver bullet, but it can be like what when pointed in the right direction?**
A) A guided missile
B) A heat-seeking missile
C) A bullet train
D) A sniper rifle

192. **What does the Scrum framework help to transform?**
A) Outmoded business practices
B) Only software development practices

C) Marketing strategies

D) Financial operations

193. What does Scrum encourage for developers and stakeholders?

A) A competitive environment

B) A better life and extreme business value

C) A strict hierarchy

D) Detailed documentation

194. When was the first Scrum project initiated?

A) 1983

B) 1986

C) 1993

D) 2001

195. Which of the following companies has NOT been mentioned as using Scrum?

A) Google

B) Amazon

C) Microsoft

D) Ericsson

196. What is "The Scrum Guide"?

A) A novel about rugby

B) A manual for Scrum at Scrum, Inc.

C) The official guide defining the Scrum framework

D) An appendix in the manual

197. What is the primary focus of Agile principles?

A) Extensive upfront planning

B) Building working software quickly

C) Long-term project milestones
D) Comprehensive documentation

198. **What does Scrum structure development into?**
A) Phases
B) Milestones
C) Sprints
D) Stages

199. **What are the Scrum Papers?**
A) A set of rugby rules
B) A collection of Scrum case studies
C) Papers and compendiums used at Scrum, Inc.
D) A list of certified Scrum practitioners

200. **What is a common outcome for teams that effectively implement Scrum?**
A) No change in productivity
B) Decreased morale
C) Improvements in productivity and morale
D) Increased bureaucracy

201. **What is one characteristic of Sprints in Scrum?**
A) They can be extended if needed
B) Their duration is determined by the team
C) They end on a specific date whether work is completed or not
D) They are only for software projects

202. **When was Scrum formalized into a framework?**
A) 1983
B) 1995
C) 2001
D) 1993

Product Questions

203. **Where can one find the fully defined Scrum framework?**
    A) In the Harvard Business Review
    B) At www.scrum.org
    C) In "The Scrum Papers"
    D) At Easel Corporation

204. **What is the goal of the daily Scrum meeting?**
    A) To report progress to stakeholders
    B) To discuss personal matters
    C) To re-plan work to achieve the Sprint's goals
    D) To extend the Sprint duration

205. **How often are Sprints conducted in Scrum?**
    A) Once a year
    B) One after the other without breaks
    C) Whenever the team decides
    D) At the end of every project

206. **What does the term "potentially shippable" refer to in Scrum?**
    A) A product ready for release
    B) A product that needs further testing
    C) A product in the early stages of development
    D) A product that has been shipped

207. **Who maintains and helps the Scrum Guide to emerge further?**
    A) Professors Takeuchi and Nonaka
    B) Bill Gates and Paul Allen
    C) Ken Schwaber and Jeff Sutherland
    D) The team at Scrum, Inc.

208. **What is a Scrum team encouraged to build?**
　A) A detailed plan
　B) A community of stakeholders
　C) An extensive documentation
　D) A hierarchical structure

209. **According to the text, why is Scrum powerful?**
　A) Because it is complex
　B) Because it is simple and powerful
　C) Because it is a traditional method
　D) Because it requires no inspection or adaptation

210. **What does the Scrum framework require after a development step?**
　A) No further action
　B) Immediate release of the product
　C) An inspection and adaptation of the product and practices
　D) A move to the next phase without review

211. **What is the primary function of the Product Owner in Scrum?**
　A) Removing organizational impediments
　B) Writing detailed requirements documents
　C) Prioritizing the Product Backlog
　D) Testing the end product

212. **How long are Sprints in a Scrum project typically?**
　A) 1-2 days
　B) 1-4 weeks
　C) 2-6 months
　D) 1 year

213. **What is the purpose of the Sprint Planning Meeting?**
    A) To discuss the team's performance
    B) To assign tasks to team members
    C) To select items from the Product Backlog for the upcoming Sprint
    D) To review work completed in the previous Sprint

214. **What is the Sprint Backlog?**
    A) A list of all the product features
    B) A prioritized list of customer requirements
    C) A set of granulated steps for items selected for the Sprint
    D) The detailed plan for the entire project

215. **How long does the Daily Stand-Up Meeting last?**
    A) As long as necessary to cover all issues
    B) 15 minutes
    C) 1 hour
    D) 30 minutes

216. **Who attends the Sprint Review?**
    A) Only the Scrum Team
    B) Product Owner, Team Members, Scrum Master, and stakeholders
    C) Customers and executives only
    D) Quality Assurance team

217. **What is the goal of the Sprint Retrospective?**
    A) To plan the next Sprint
    B) To discuss what's working and what's not
    C) To present the completed work to stakeholders
    D) To re-prioritize the Product Backlog

Product Questions

218. The traditional "Waterfall" model of software development is characterized by what approach?
A) Iterative and incremental
B) Sequential life cycle
C) Flexible and adaptive
D) Concurrent development

219. In the Waterfall model, when is creativity typically expected to occur?
A) Throughout the process
B) At the beginning of the release cycle
C) After the testing phase
D) Just before the product launch

220. What is a significant drawback of using written documents in the Waterfall approach?
A) They are time-consuming to create
B) They encourage too much creativity.
C) They are often not read or are misunderstood.
D) They are too brief to capture complex ideas.

221. When do valuable insights into the product typically emerge in the Waterfall model?
A) During the planning phase
B) In the middle of the release cycle
C) At the end of the release cycle
D) After the product launch

222. What is a fundamental problem with the Waterfall model related to planning?
A) It allows too much flexibility.
B) It lacks a structured approach.

Product Questions

C) It assumes humans can predict the future accurately.

D) It encourages too frequent changes.

223. **How does the Waterfall model affect the morale of the team members?**

A) It leads to high job satisfaction

B) It creates an adversarial relationship between team members.

C) It fosters a collaborative environment.

D) It encourages creative freedom.

224. **What tends to be the result of a rigid, change-resistant process like the Waterfall model?**

A) Highly innovative products

B) Mediocre products

C) Products that exceed customer expectations

D) Extremely flexible products

225. **What is a common reaction to the problems experienced with the Waterfall model?**

A) To adopt a different model like Scrum

B) To increase flexibility and allow more changes

C) To plan more, document more, and resist change more

D) To reduce the amount of documentation

226. **What was the first company to create a Scrum team?**

A) Google

B) Adobe

C) Easel Corporation

D) Microsoft

227. **In Scrum, what is the maximum length of a Sprint?**

A) 2 weeks

B) 4 weeks

C) 1 month
D) 6 weeks

228. **Who formalized the Scrum framework in 1995?**
    A) Dr. Jeff Sutherland and Ken Schwaber
    B) Professors Takeuchi and Nonaka
    C) The Easel Corporation team
    D) The first Scrum team

229. **Which meeting in Scrum focuses on what will be developed in the next Sprint?**
    A) Daily Stand-up
    B) Sprint Review
    C) Sprint Retrospective
    D) Sprint Planning Meeting

230. **Who is responsible for maximizing ROI in a Scrum project?**
    A) The Scrum Master
    B) The Team
    C) The Product Owner
    D) The stakeholders

231. **What key practice does the Scrum Team engage in daily?**
    A) Sprint Retrospective
    B) Sprint Review
    C) Daily Stand-Up Meeting
    D) Backlog Grooming

232. **How is traditional software development commonly known?**
    A) The Scrum
    B) The Sprint

C) The Waterfall
D) The Agile

233. What is a significant theme in Scrum regarding product development?
A) Detailed upfront planning
B) Inspect and adapt
C) Adherence to a strict plan
D) Avoiding customer input

234. Scrum emphasizes a working product at the end of each Sprint that is really "done." Which of the following is not a characteristic of "done" in software development?
A) Integrated
B) Fully tested
C) Potentially shippable
D) Fully documented

235. How are Scrum projects driven?
A) By a detailed specification document
B) By a product vision created by the Product Owner
C) By a project manager's direction
D) By customer complaints

236. What is the Product Backlog?
A) A list of completed tasks
B) A prioritized list of requirements
C) A record of daily meetings
D) A collection of Sprint Retrospectives

237. Who is responsible for removing impediments that may block the Scrum Team's progress?
A) The stakeholders

B) The Product Owner
C) The Scrum Master
D) The Team

238. What is the recommended size for a Scrum Team?
A) 3-5 people
B) 5-9 people
C) 10-15 people
D) 20-25 people

239. In Scrum, what does the term "potentially shippable" refer to?
A) A product ready to be shipped at the end of the project
B) A product feature that has been approved by the stakeholders
C) A product or increment that is ready for use at the end of each Sprint
D) A product that has passed all tests but has not yet been released

240. Who makes up the Scrum Team?
A) Product Owner, Scrum Master, and Team Members
B) Project Manager and Team Members
C) Stakeholders and Executives
D) Customers and Users

241. What is the primary characteristic of Sprints in the Scrum framework?
A) They have variable durations
B) They are extended if the work is not completed
C) They are time-boxed and fixed in duration
D) They co-occur with other project activities

242. **How does Scrum handle customer requirements during a Sprint?**
    A) Customers can change requirements anytime during the Sprint
    B) Requirements are selected at the end of the Sprint
    C) Requirements are fixed and selected at the beginning of the Sprint
    D) The development team randomly chooses requirements

243. **What is the critical outcome of a Sprint in Scrum?**
    A) Detailed documentation of completed tasks
    B) A partially integrated product
    C) Code that is integrated, thoroughly tested, and potentially shippable
    D) A comprehensive project status report

244. **Which principle is central to Scrum's philosophy of continuous improvement?**
    A) Incremental development
    B) Fixed project scope
    C) Inspect and adapt
    D) Long-term planning

245. **What is the fundamental goal of Agile development methods like Scrum?**
    A) Following a strict plan without deviation
    B) Building extensive documentation upfront
    C) Empowering cross-functional teams to make decisions
    D) Avoiding customer involvement until the end of the project

246. **What analogy is drawn between Scrum and the game of Rugby?**
    A) Both involve strict hierarchical structures

B) Both emphasize compartmentalization by function
C) Both utilize rapid iteration and continuous input
D) Both focus on lengthy planning phases

247. Who introduced the term "Scrum" in the context of product development?

A) Ken Schwaber
B) Dr. Jeff Sutherland
C) Professors Takeuchi and Nonaka
D) Easel Corporation

248. What is the overarching message conveyed by the text regarding Scrum's impact?

A) Scrum is a complex framework with limited practical application
B) Scrum has revolutionized product development with its simplicity and effectiveness
C) Scrum is only suitable for small-scale projects and startups
D) Scrum's influence is limited to a few niche industries

249. Which of the following companies is NOT mentioned as a user of Scrum?

A) Google
B) Lockheed Martin
C) Apple
D) Cisco

250. What is the ultimate goal of Scrum?

A) Maximizing profits for shareholders
B) Delivering extreme business value to customers
C) Strict adherence to predetermined project plans
D) Minimizing team creativity and autonomy

Answers

Answers

1. B) Confusion

Explanation: If a change initiative is missing a clear Vision according to the Knoster Model, the likely outcome would be confusion among the stakeholders and team members about the direction and purpose of the change.

2. B) Be subjective and biased

Explanation: As a Scrum Master, being subjective and biased is not desirable when considering the 6 Facilitation Factors. Facilitation should aim for neutrality and objectivity to ensure fair and effective collaboration within the team.

3. B) Professional Scrum Master I certification

Explanation: With a total skill assessment score between 25 and 29, a potential development opportunity for a Scrum Master could be obtaining the Professional Scrum Master I certification to enhance their skills and knowledge in Scrum practices.

4. A) Teaching the team to practice Scrum

Explanation: The role of the Scrum Master as "the Model" primarily involves teaching the team to practice Scrum by demonstrating the principles and values of Scrum in their actions and behaviors.

5. D) 4

Answers

Explanation: If a Scrum Master is skilled at facilitating Scrum events without referring to a checklist, this should be scored as a 4, indicating a high level of proficiency in that skill area.

6. B) Encouraging the team member's autonomy and purpose

Explanation: By empowering the team members to take ownership of their work and connecting their tasks to a broader purpose or vision, the Scrum Master can help reignite their enthusiasm and commitment. This approach fosters a sense of responsibility and significance, which can boost the team member's willingness to contribute actively to the team's goals.

7. B) To implement and manage change effectively

Explanation: The primary responsibility of the Scrum Master as "the Change Agent" is to implement and manage change effectively within the team and organization, ensuring the successful adoption of Agile practices.

8. D) False Start

Explanation: When a change initiative lacks the necessary skills, according to the Knoster Model, the likely result would be a false start, indicating an unsuccessful attempt to initiate the change due to insufficient skills.

9. B) Somewhat Disagree

Explanation: If the team does not regularly conduct product demos to stakeholders, a Scrum Master might somewhat disagree with this

Answers

practice, as regular product demos are essential for gathering feedback and ensuring stakeholder involvement.

10. D) False Start

Explanation: False Start is not an outcome of missing Resources when managing complex change. Frustration, confusion, and resistance are more likely outcomes.

11. B) Power and Interest Matrix

Explanation: The primary tool used in traditional project management for stakeholder management is the Power and Interest Matrix, which helps analyze stakeholders based on their power and interest in the project.

12. A) Scrum Master

Explanation: Typically, both the Scrum Master and the Product Owner are responsible for stakeholder management in a Scrum team. Still, the Scrum Master often takes the lead in facilitating communication and addressing stakeholder concerns.

13. B) Ignoring the stakeholders completely

Explanation: A common mistake Scrum Masters often make regarding stakeholders is ignoring them completely, which can lead to misunderstandings and a lack of support for the project.

14. B) 2 PDUs

Answers

Explanation: Participants can earn 2 PDUs by participating in each Cprime web seminar, which can contribute to their professional development and certification requirements.

15. C) Scaled Agile Program Consultant (SPC)

Explanation: Mr. Eugene Lai does not hold the Scaled Agile Program Consultant (SPC) certification among the given options.

16. B) Validating alignment to business strategy

Explanation: The focus of Lean Portfolio Management, as offered by Cprime, is on validating alignment to business strategy, ensuring that Agile practices and initiatives support the organization's overall goals.

17. B) Providing an in-depth understanding of the ScrumMaster role

Explanation: The primary objective of the Advanced Certified ScrumMaster (A-CSM) course is to provide participants with an in-depth understanding of the ScrumMaster role, enhancing their skills and capabilities in facilitating Agile practices within teams.

18. C) Traditional Waterfall/SDLC

Explanation: Traditional Waterfall/SDLC is not included in Cprime's Agile Solutions, as Cprime primarily focuses on Agile methodologies and practices for software development and project management.

19. C) 6

Answers

Explanation: Mr. Eugene Lai has architected 6 corporate PMOs according to the provided information.

20. C) A high level of commitment and a growth mindset

Explanation: Transitioning from an experienced Scrum Master to an Advanced Scrum Master requires a high level of commitment and a growth mindset to continuously improve skills and adapt to new challenges in Agile environments.

21. C) To inspect the team's practices and make improvements

Explanation: The Sprint Retrospective aims to inspect the team's practices, processes, and interactions during the Sprint and identify opportunities for improvement in the next Sprint.

22. B) To refine and prioritize backlog items

Explanation: Product Backlog Grooming is the process of refining and prioritizing backlog so they are ready for selection in future Sprints.

23. B) Provides flexibility to handle change requests

Explanation: Scrum provides flexibility to handle change requests and adapt to evolving requirements throughout the project.

24. A) Facilitating the Daily Scrum

Answers

Explanation: Facilitating the Daily Scrum is typically the responsibility of the Scrum Master, not the Product Owner. The Product Owner focuses on managing the product backlog, maximizing its value, and prioritizing backlog items.

25. C) Ensuring the Scrum framework is followed

Explanation: The Scrum Master is responsible for ensuring that the Scrum framework is followed and helping the team understand and implement Scrum practices effectively.

26. A) An ordered list of everything needed in the product

Explanation: The Product Backlog is an ordered list of all features, enhancements, bug fixes, and other work needed to achieve the product vision.

27. B) A timeboxed iteration of one month or less

Explanation: The Sprint in Scrum is a timeboxed iteration of one month or less during which a potentially shippable product increment is created.

28. D) The sum of all Product Backlog items completed during a Sprint and all previous Sprints

Explanation: An Increment in Scrum is the sum of all Product Backlog items completed during a Sprint and all previous Sprints, representing the work done and the progress made on the product.

Answers

29. A) A project with a well-defined scope and few expected changes

Explanation: A project with a well-defined scope and few expected changes may benefit from using traditional methods over Scrum, as Scrum is best suited for projects with evolving requirements and frequent changes.

30. B) To make sure all parties understand their roles and responsibilities

Explanation: Scrum training ensures that all team members understand their roles and responsibilities, fostering effective collaboration and adherence to Scrum principles and practices.

31. B) To facilitate Scrum events and ensure the framework is followed

Explanation: The primary role of the Scrum Master is to facilitate Scrum events, coach the team on Scrum practices, and ensure that the Scrum framework is followed effectively.

32. B) To maintain and prioritize the Product Backlog

Explanation: The primary responsibility of the Product Owner in Scrum is to maintain and prioritize the Product Backlog, ensuring that it reflects the vision, goals, and priorities of the product.

33. C) Selected items for the upcoming Sprint

Answers

Explanation: The Sprint Backlog consists of selected items from the Product Backlog that the Development Team plans to work on during the upcoming Sprint.

34. D) It varies based on project complexity

Explanation: The typical Sprint duration in Scrum varies based on the project complexity and the team's preferences, but it is generally between one to four weeks.

35. C) To plan work for the next 24 hours

Explanation: The purpose of the Daily Scrum meeting is for the Development Team to plan their work for the next 24 hours, discuss progress, and identify any impediments.

36. B) Anytime during the Sprint as needed

Explanation: During the sprint, circumstances may change, new information may arise, or the team may encounter unexpected challenges that require adjustments to the Sprint Backlog. Therefore, it's essential for the team to have the flexibility to update the Sprint Backlog as necessary to reflect the current state of the sprint and to ensure they can achieve the sprint goal.

37. C) The Development Team

Explanation: The Definition of Done is created by the Development Team and defines the criteria that must be met for a product backlog item to be considered complete.

Answers

38. B) The sum of all Product Backlog items completed during a Sprint

Explanation: An Increment is the result of the work done during a sprint that adds to the value delivered to the product. Each Increment must be potentially shippable, meaning it should be in a usable state and meet the Definition of Done, ensuring that it can be released if needed. This incremental delivery approach allows for regular progress checks and the ability to adapt to changing requirements and feedback.

39. D) The Whole Scrum Team

Explanation: The Sprint Planning meeting is attended by the whole Scrum Team, which includes the Product Owner, the Scrum Master, and the Development Team.

40. B) At the Sprint Planning meeting

Explanation: The Sprint Backlog is created during the Sprint Planning meeting, where the Development Team selects the Product Backlog items they forecast they can complete in the upcoming Sprint.

41. B) The Product Owner

Explanation: The Product Owner is responsible for prioritizing the Product Backlog. They ensure that the most valuable and important items are worked on first, aligning the team's work with the overall product vision and stakeholder needs.

42. B) To demonstrate the work done during the Sprint

Answers

Explanation: The primary purpose of the Sprint Review is to demonstrate the Increment to stakeholders and gather feedback to inform future development.

43. C) To reflect on the past Sprint and identify improvements

Explanation: The Sprint Retrospective aims to reflect on the past Sprint, identify what went well and what could be improved, and then create a plan for implementing improvements in the next Sprint.

44. B) It is self-organizing and cross-functional

Explanation: A Scrum Team is characterized by its ability to self-organize and possess all the skills necessary within the team to complete the work without depending on others outside the team. This autonomy and diverse skill set enable them to manage their work and deliver value efficiently.

45. C) To refine the Product Backlog items and ensure they are ready for future Sprints

Explanation: The Backlog Grooming session aims to refine the Product Backlog Grooming session, ensuring they are clear, actionable, and ready for selection in future Sprints.

46. C) Continuously throughout the project

Explanation: The Product Backlog is continuously updated throughout the project as new information emerges, priorities change, and stakeholder feedback is received.

Answers

47.   C) The Burndown Chart

Explanation: The Burndown Chart monitors Sprint progress by tracking the remaining work in the Sprint Backlog over time.

48.   C) The Product Owner

Explanation: Any stakeholder, including the Product Owner, stakeholders external to the Scrum Team, or even the Development Team itself, has the authority to cancel a Sprint if it's deemed necessary.

49.   C) The Sprint Planning Meeting

Explanation: The Sprint Planning meeting marks the start of a new Sprint, where the Scrum Team collaboratively plans the work to be done during the Sprint.

50.   C) It is an ordered list of everything that might be needed in the product

Explanation: The Product Backlog is an ordered list that contains all the features, enhancements, bug fixes, and other requirements that might be needed for the product. It is continuously refined and reprioritized.

51.   C) To ensure the meeting is productive and stays within the time box

Explanation: The Scrum Master's role during the Daily Scrum is to facilitate the meeting, ensure it stays within the timebox, and remove

Answers

any impediments that hinder the Development Team's progress. The Scrum Master does not assign tasks during the Daily Scrum.

52.   B) 30 days

Explanation: The maximum duration for a Sprint in Scrum is 30 days, although shorter durations are often recommended for increased agility and feedback.

53.   C) By the Development Team itself

Explanation: In Scrum, the Development Team members self-organize and collectively decide how to accomplish the work best agreed upon in the Sprint Backlog.

54.   C) Delivering value through iterative progress

Explanation: The main focus of the Scrum framework is on delivering value to the customer through iterative progress, enabling adaptation to changing requirements and maximizing transparency and collaboration.

55.   B) A high-level definition of a requirement, focusing on the value it provides to the customer

Explanation: A User Story in the context of Scrum is a high-level definition of a requirement, typically written from the perspective of an end-user or customer, focusing on the value it provides.

56.   D) Gantt Chart

Answers

Explanation: A Gantt Chart is not a Scrum Artifact. Scrum Artifacts include the Product Backlog, Sprint Backlog, and Increment.

57. B) The Sprint Goal and Sprint Backlog

Explanation: The outcome of the Sprint Planning meeting includes defining the Sprint Goal and creating the Sprint Backlog, which lists the Product Backlog items selected for the Sprint.

58. C) By the order of importance and value

Explanation: Product Backlog items should be sorted by the order of importance and value, with the most valuable items at the top of the list. This helps that the Development Team works on the most valuable features first.

59. C) The Scrum Team and any interested stakeholders

Explanation: The Sprint Review is attended by the Scrum Team (Product Owner, Scrum Master, and Development Team) and any interested stakeholders, such as customers, users, or management.

60. B) To define the business purpose and objective of the Sprint

Explanation: The primary purpose of the Sprint Goal is to define the business purpose and objective of the Sprint, providing a clear focus for the Development Team and aligning their efforts towards a common goal.

Answers

61. C) To maximize the value of the product and work of the Development Team

Explanation: The role of the Product Owner in a Scrum team is to maximize product by managing and prioritizing the Product Backlog, ensuring that the Development Team is working on the most valuable items.

62. B) Three

Explanation: In a Scrum project, three roles are defined: Product Owner, Scrum Master, and Development Team.

63. D) The Product Owner, Scrum Master, and the Development Team

Explanation: The term "Scrum Team" refers to the Product Owner, Scrum Master, and the Development Team collectively, who work together to deliver increments of a product.

64. B) Scrum Master

Explanation: The Scrum Master is considered a 'servant-leader' in Scrum, facilitating the Scrum process and serving the Scrum Team by removing impediments and fostering an environment of collaboration and self-organization.

65. B) 3-9

Explanation: Typically, a Scrum Development Team consists of 3-9 individuals who have the skills necessary to deliver a potentially shippable product increment at the end of each Sprint.

Answers

66. B) Product Backlog

Explanation: The primary planning tool in Scrum is the Product Backlog, which contains a prioritized list of all desired work on the project.

67. A) Yes, it is recommended.

Explanation: Yes, individuals in a Scrum project are recommended to have multiple roles, such as being a Development Team member and a Scrum Master.

68. A) Self-organized and cross-functional

Explanation: The two essential characteristics of a Scrum Team are that it is self-organized,

meaning the team members collectively decide how to accomplish their work and cross-functional, it has all the skills necessary to deliver the product increment.

69. B) Scrum Master

Explanation: The Scrum Master removes impediments in a Scrum project, ensuring that the Development Team can work efficiently and without obstacles.

70. D) Full-time on a single project

Answers

Explanation: The recommended way for Development Team members to work on projects is full-time on a single project, ensuring their focus and commitment to delivering the Sprint goals.

71.   A) The individual who performs the task

Explanation: The individual who performs the task is accountable for the tasks in the Sprint Backlog, as they are responsible for completing the work.

72.   C) Product Owner

Explanation: The Product Owner sets the order of items in the Product Backlog based on their value and priority to the product.

73.   B) False

Explanation: False. The Product Owner can be from the customer's organization, but it's not a strict requirement. They represent the stakeholders and are responsible for maximizing product value.

74.   C) Should not change often

Explanation: The composition of a Development Team should not change often to maintain stability and effectiveness. However, it can change to improve performance or adapt to changing project needs.

75.   D) No, it eliminates their role entirely

Explanation: Scrum does not prescribe a specific role for traditional project managers. Instead, it distributes its responsibilities among the

Answers

Product Owner, Scrum Master, and Development Team, emphasizing self-organization and collaboration over hierarchical management.

76. B) Yes, but there must be a single representative

Explanation: While it's possible to have a committee for the Product Owner role, there must be a committee representative with authority to make decisions on behalf of the stakeholders.

77. B) To ensure each item is well understood by stakeholders

Explanation: A key responsibility of the Product Owner regarding the Product Backlog is to ensure that each item is well understood by stakeholders, including the Development Team, to facilitate effective prioritization and decision-making.

78. B) Scrum Master

Explanation: The Scrum Master is responsible for coaching the Product Owner, helping them understand and effectively perform their role within the Scrum framework.

79. A) True

Explanation: True. The Development Team in Scrum should be cross-functional, meaning it includes all the skills necessary to deliver a potentially shippable product increment, which may include roles like designer, tester, and team leader.

80. B) Sprint Review

Answers

Explanation: The Sprint Review demonstrates completed work to the customer or stakeholders and gathers feedback for future iterations.

81. C) Change should occur between Sprints to minimize disruption

Explanation: If the Scrum Team composition needs to change, it's recommended that the change occurs between Sprints to minimize disruption to ongoing work.

82. C) The Product Owner

Explanation: The Product Owner is responsible for prioritizing the Product Backlog based on value, ensuring that the most valuable items are at the top for implementation by the Development Team.

83. B) A potentially releasable part of the final product

Explanation: In Scrum, an Increment is a potentially releasable part of the final product produced at the end of each Sprint and includes all the completed and "Done" Product Backlog items.

84. B) Scrum Master

Explanation: The Scrum Master ensures that the Scrum framework is correctly implemented by coaching the Scrum Team, facilitating Scrum events, and removing impediments to the team's progress.

85. A) Full-time status is recommended for maximum focus and productivity

Answers

Explanation: Having Scrum Team members work full-time ensures they can fully dedicate their efforts and attention to the team's goals, enhancing collaboration, communication, and overall productivity.

86. A) Progress toward a Sprint goal

Explanation: A Burndown chart monitors the progress of a Scrum Team towards achieving the Sprint goal by tracking the remaining work in the Sprint backlog over time.

87. B) To resolve or remove them

Explanation: The Scrum Master's role regarding impediments is to facilitate their resolution or removal, ensuring that the Development Team can work smoothly towards achieving the Sprint goal.

88. B) 5-12

Explanation: The size range of a Scrum Team typically includes 5 to 12 individuals, including all three roles: Product Owner, Scrum Master, and Development Team members.

89. C) The Product Owner

Explanation: The Product Owner is responsible for measuring the performance of a Scrum project, particularly in terms of whether the product increment delivered meets the stakeholders' expectations and requirements.

90. C) The team discusses improvements for the next Sprint

Answers

Explanation: The Sprint Retrospective is a meeting where the Scrum Team reflects on their performance during the Sprint and identifies opportunities for improvement in the upcoming Sprints.

91. B) 1 month

Explanation: The maximum duration for a Sprint in Scrum is typically one month, although shorter durations, such as two weeks, are also common.

92. C) Product Owner

Explanation: The Product Owner is responsible for maximizing product value by ensuring that the Development Team works on the most valuable items in the Product Backlog.

93. C) Quality Assurance Manager

Explanation: While Quality Assurance may be involved in the development process, it is not a standard role in Scrum. The standard roles are Product Owner, Scrum Master, and Development Team.

94. B) To plan the work for the next Sprint

Explanation: The purpose of the Sprint Planning event is for the Scrum Team to plan the work that will be undertaken in the upcoming Sprint based on the prioritized items in the Product Backlog.

95. B) 15 minutes

Answers

Explanation: The Daily Scrum is a timeboxed event in Scrum that typically lasts 15 minutes, where the Development Team members synchronize their activities and plan their work for the next 24 hours.

96. C) Re-estimate and carry forward to the next Sprint

Explanation: If an item cannot be completed by the end of the Sprint, it should be re-estimated and carried forward to the next Sprint Planning meeting.

97. B) Scrum Master

Explanation: The Scrum Master is responsible for facilitating the Sprint Retrospective, where the Scrum Team reflects on their process and identifies areas for improvement.

98. A) The items completed during a single Sprint

Explanation: The Increment in Scrum refers to the sum of all the Product Backlog items completed during a Sprint and all previous Sprints, providing tangible value to the product.

99. D) Any stakeholder

Explanation: Any stakeholder, including the Product Owner, Scrum Master, or even team members, can request the cancellation of a Sprint if it no longer makes sense given the circumstances.

100. B) To ensure regularity and minimize complexity

Answers

Explanation: Timeboxing events in Scrum ensures regularity, provides a cadence for the team, and helps minimize the complexity of planning and execution.

101. A) 2 hours

Explanation: For a one-month Sprint, the typical duration of a Sprint Review is around 2 hours, but this can vary depending on the complexity of the product and the amount of feedback to be discussed.

102. B) 10%

Explanation: The maximum recommended time for Product Backlog grooming activities during a Sprint is around 10% of the Sprint duration, ensuring that the Product Backlog remains refined and ready for future Sprints.

103. B) To track remaining work in the Sprint

Explanation: A Burndown Chart in Scrum is used to visually track the remaining work in the Sprint backlog over time, helping the team monitor their progress towards completing the Sprint goal.

104. D) An objective that will be met within the Sprint through the implementation of the Product Backlog

Explanation: The Sprint Goal is a short statement that describes the objective to be achieved during the Sprint, guiding the Development Team in their work towards delivering a potentially shippable product increment.

Answers

105. D) Sprint Retrospective

Explanation: The Sprint Retrospective is specifically designed for process improvement, where the Scrum Team reflects on their process and identifies ways to make improvements in future Sprints.

106. C) They are re-estimated and returned to the Product Backlog

Explanation: Incomplete Product Backlog items at the end of a Sprint are re-estimated and returned to the Product Backlog for prioritization in future Sprints.

107. B) Scrum Master

Explanation: In the Daily Scrum meeting, the Scrum Master facilitates the discussion. The Scrum Master ensures that the meeting stays focused, remains within the time box, and encourages all team members to participate actively. Their role is to facilitate collaboration and help remove any obstacles that may hinder the team's progress.

108. B) To facilitate the meeting

Explanation: The role of the Scrum Master during the Sprint Review is to facilitate the meeting, ensuring that the stakeholders provide feedback on the Increment and that any potential changes to the Product Backlog are discussed.

109. A) Anytime during the Sprint

Answers

Explanation: Changes to the Sprint Backlog can be made anytime during the Sprint, as long as they do not endanger the Sprint goal and are agreed upon by the Scrum Team.

110. C) Product Owner

Explanation: The Product Owner is responsible for ordering the items in the Product Backlog based on their value, ensuring that the Development Team works on the most valuable items first.

111. C) It meets the criteria defined in the "Definition of Done."

Explanation: A Product Backlog item is considered "Done" when it meets the criteria defined in the "Definition of Done," indicating that it is potentially shippable and meets the quality standards of the product.

112. C) Works to remove the impediment

Explanation: The Scrum Master works to remove impediments that block the progress of the Development Team, ensuring that they can work effectively towards achieving the Sprint goal.

113. B) 3-9

Explanation: The recommended number of people in the Development Team typically ranges from 3 to 9 individuals, although smaller or larger teams may also be effective depending on the context.

Answers

114. C) A coach and facilitator who ensures the Scrum process is followed

Explanation: The Scrum Master acts as a coach and facilitator within the Scrum Team, ensuring that the team understands and follows the Scrum framework and helping to remove any obstacles that may hinder their progress.

115. C) Re-plan the Sprint

Explanation: If the composition of the Development Team changes during a Sprint, it may be necessary to re-plan the Sprint to ensure that the team can still effectively work towards achieving the Sprint goal.

116. D) Delivering valuable product increments

Explanation: The main focus of Scrum is to deliver valuable product increments iteratively and incrementally, ensuring that the product evolves based on feedback and changing requirements.

117. C) All members of the Scrum Team

Explanation: The Sprint Retrospective is attended by all members of the Scrum Team, including the Product Owner, Scrum Master, and Development Team members, to reflect on the Sprint and identify areas for improvement.

118. C) Sprint Backlog

Answers

Explanation: The primary artifact created during Sprint Planning is the Sprint Backlog, which lists all the tasks the Development Team will perform during the Sprint to achieve the Sprint Goal.

119. C) Continuously throughout the project

Explanation: The Product Backlog is created at the beginning of the project and continuously maintained throughout its duration to reflect changes in requirements, priorities, and stakeholder feedback.

120. B) To participate and provide updates

Explanation: The role of the Product Owner during the Daily Scrum is to participate as a member of the Development Team, providing updates on the progress and any relevant information.

121. C) Individuals and interactions

Explanation: The main focus of the Agile Manifesto is on individuals and interactions over processes and tools, emphasizing the importance of collaboration and communication within the development team.

122. D) The Product Owner manages the day-to-day activities of the Team

Explanation: This statement is false. The Product Owner is responsible for maximizing the value of the product and managing the Product Backlog, not for managing the day-to-day activities of the Development Team.

Answers

123. C) The Product Owner

Explanation: The Product Owner is responsible for creating and maintaining the Product Backlog, ensuring that it reflects the latest priorities and requirements of the stakeholders.

124. A) 15 minutes

Explanation: The Daily Scrum meeting is timeboxed to a maximum of 15 minutes, ensuring that it remains focused and efficient while providing the necessary updates and coordination.

125. B) To provide a buffer for unplanned work

Explanation: Slack in Scrum provides a buffer for unplanned work, allowing the team to handle unexpected issues or changes without affecting the Sprint goal.

126. D) There is no equivalent role

Explanation: In Scrum, there is no role equivalent to a traditional Project Manager. The responsibilities traditionally associated with a Project Manager are distributed among the Product Owner, Scrum Master, and Development Team.

127. B) Sprint Backlog

Explanation: The Sprint Backlog provides information about the work to be performed in the Sprint, including the tasks necessary to achieve the Sprint Goal.

Answers

128. C) The criteria for accepting work as completed

Explanation: The Definition of "Done" in Scrum signifies the criteria that a product increment must meet to be considered completed and potentially shippable.

129. C) Reflect on the Scrum process and improve it

Explanation: Self-assessment in Scrum is important to reflect on the Scrum process and identify areas for improvement, contributing to the continuous improvement of the team's effectiveness.

130. A) Requirements change frequently

Explanation: Scrum is more suitable than traditional methods when requirements change frequently, as it provides flexibility and adaptability to accommodate changing needs and priorities.

131. C) A maximum duration for a Scrum event

Explanation: A timebox in Scrum refers to a maximum duration set for a Scrum event, ensuring that the event remains focused and efficient.

132. A) Sprint Burndown Chart

Explanation: The Sprint Burndown Chart helps to monitor the Sprint's progress by visually tracking the remaining work in the Sprint backlog over time.

133. C) The Product Owner

Answers

Explanation:

The Product Owner is responsible for maximizing the value of the product by ensuring that the Development Team works on the most valuable items in the Product Backlog.

134. C) It is completely eliminated

Explanation: The traditional project manager role in Scrum is generally eliminated as the responsibilities are distributed among the Scrum Master, Product Owner, and Development Team.

135. B) Contingency reserve

Explanation: The concept of 'Slack' in Scrum is most similar to the traditional project management practice of Contingency Reserve, providing a buffer for unexpected events or changes.

136. B) Prescribed and timeboxed

Explanation: Scrum events are prescribed, meaning they have a set structure and purpose, and they are timeboxed, meaning they have a maximum duration to ensure focus and efficiency.

137. C) Cross-functionality and self-organization

Explanation: The Development Team in Scrum is characterized by cross-functionality, meaning they possess all the skills necessary to deliver a product increment, and self-organization, meaning they determine how to accomplish their work without external direction.

Answers

138. C) The Scrum Master, Product Owner, and Development Team

Explanation: The Sprint Planning meeting is attended by the entire Scrum Team, including the Scrum Master, Product Owner, and Development Team, to collaborate on selecting and planning the work to be done in the upcoming Sprint.

139. C) Using artifacts like the Sprint Burndown Chart

Explanation: In Scrum, progress toward a goal is monitored using various artifacts, with the Sprint Burndown Chart being a key tool. This chart visually represents the remaining work in the sprint, allowing the team to track their progress and make necessary adjustments.

140. B) Scrum is difficult, complex, and challenging to implement without proper training.

Explanation: Proper training and understanding of Scrum principles and practices are essential for successful implementation, making this statement true.

141. C) To cover specific Learning Objectives based on the Scrum Guide and Agile Manifesto

Explanation: The primary purpose of a Certified ScrumMaster (CSM) course is to cover specific Learning Objectives based on the Scrum Guide and Agile Manifesto, providing participants with a comprehensive understanding of Scrum principles and practices.

142. B) Scrum Event Planning

Answers

Explanation: Scrum Event Planning is not a category of the CSM Learning Objectives. The categories include Agile Coaching, Service to the Development Team, and Service to the Organization.

143.   B) A framework

Explanation: According to the Learning Objectives, Scrum is primarily a framework, providing a structure and guidelines for managing complex projects.

144.   C) Efficiency

Explanation: Efficiency is not a Scrum value. The Scrum values are Commitment, Courage, Focus, Openness, and Respect.

145.   C) Three to nine people

Explanation: The maximum recommended size for a Development Team in Scrum is typically three to nine people to enable effective collaboration and communication.

146.   D) All of the above

Explanation: Having a single Product Owner simplifies communication, ensures a clear line of authority, and helps avoid decision-making delays.

147.   A) Inspection, Adaptation, Transparency

Answers

Explanation: The three pillars of empirical process control in Scrum are Inspection, Adaptation, and Transparency, which form the basis for continuous improvement.

148. C) Both A and B

Explanation: The Scrum Master facilitates the Daily Scrum, ensuring the conversation flows smoothly and follows the agenda of the three questions.

149. B) A potentially releasable product increment

Explanation: The outcome of every Sprint in Scrum is a potentially releasable product increment, meaning it meets the Definition of Done and could be released to stakeholders.

150. B) Input: "Ready" product backlog items, Outputs: Sprint goal, Sprint backlog

Explanation: The inputs to Sprint Planning include "Ready" product backlog items and the outputs include the Sprint goal and the Sprint backlog.

151. C) Offer the Sprint goal

Explanation: The Sprint goal is typically proposed by the Product Owner based on the product vision and backlog priorities. The Development Team is responsible for providing a forecast, deciding how much work to bring into the sprint, and creating Sprint Backlog items, but not for offering the Sprint goal.

Answers

152. B) To make impediments visible and work with the team to resolve them

Explanation: The role of the Scrum Master in relation to impediments is to make them visible and facilitate their resolution by working with the team.

153. C) Allocating fixed time periods for Scrum events

Explanation: Timeboxing in Scrum refers to setting fixed durations for Scrum events, such as sprints, Sprint Planning, Daily Scrums, Sprint Reviews, and Sprint Retrospectives, to promote efficiency and ensure timely progress.

154. B) It is dynamic and ordered

Explanation: The product backlog is dynamic, meaning it can change as new information emerges, and it is ordered based on priority, with the most essential items at the top.

155. C) Deadline

Explanation: A product backlog item typically includes a description, order (priority), and an estimate of effort or complexity, but it does not include a specific deadline. Deadlines are not assigned to individual backlog items within the product backlog; rather, they are managed within the context of sprint planning and delivery timelines.

156. C) The Development Team

Answers

Explanation: The responsibility of providing estimates for the product backlog items lies with the Development Team, as they are the ones who will be doing the work.

157. B) Facilitates its creation

Explanation: The Scrum Master facilitates the creation of the Definition of Done, ensuring it reflects the quality standards and criteria agreed upon by the Scrum Team.

158. A) 10% of their capacity

Explanation: The maximum amount of time the Development Team should spend on product backlog refinement is typically around 10% of their capacity to ensure they have time for Sprint work.

159. C) It ensures a high-quality product increment

Explanation: A strong Definition of Done sets clear and agreed-upon criteria that a product increment must meet before it can be considered complete. By adhering to these criteria, the Development Team ensures that each increment of work meets the desired quality standards, enhancing the overall quality of the product.

160. C) Assign tasks for the next Sprint

Explanation: Assigning tasks for the next Sprint is not the responsibility of the Product or Product Owner during the Sprint Review. The Product Owner primarily explains which product backlog items have been "Done" and collects feedback.

Answers

161. C) The consequences of poor system design or software architecture

Explanation: In Scrum, technical debt refers to the consequences of poor system design or software architecture, leading to additional work or complications in the future.

162. B) A framework provides a structure, while a methodology describes precise practices

Explanation: In Scrum, a framework offers a flexible structure that teams can adapt to their specific needs, whereas a methodology provides detailed, step-by-step practices and processes to follow. Scrum allows teams to decide how to implement the practices within its framework, making it adaptable to various contexts.

163. C) Facilitates team processes and supports the team's growth

Explanation: As a Servant-Leader, the Scrum Master facilitates team processes and supports the team's growth rather than giving orders or managing tasks.

164. C) A real-time snapshot of the Development Team's work for the Sprint

Explanation: The Sprint Backlog is an evolving document that includes all the tasks and work items the Development Team commits to completing during the Sprint. It provides a real-time overview of what the team is working on and their progress towards the Sprint Goal.

Answers

165.   C) Some organizational benefits of Scrum are lost

Explanation: Failing to adopt Scrum in its entirety can result in the team not fully realizing the benefits that Scrum offers, such as improved collaboration, transparency, and adaptability. This incomplete adoption may hinder the team's ability to deliver value effectively and may limit the organizational benefits that Scrum can bring.

166.   A) To ensure consistent product quality

Explanation: Having multiple teams working from the same product backlog with an identical Definition of Done helps maintain a consistent standard of quality across all increments produced by different teams. This consistency ensures that the product meets the expected quality criteria and reduces variability in the delivered work.

167.   B) Ensuring a shared understanding of product backlog items

Explanation: The key responsibility of the Product Owner regarding the product backlog is to ensure a shared understanding of product backlog items among the Scrum Team and stakeholders.

168.   C) Reduced morale

Explanation: Excessive time pressure applied by the Product Owner on the Development Team can lead to reduced morale among team members, impacting their motivation and productivity.

Answers

169. C) An objective set during Sprint Planning that provides guidance to the Development Team on why it is building the increment

Explanation: The Sprint Goal serves as a guiding objective for the Development Team during the Sprint, providing clarity on the purpose of the increment they are building and aligning their efforts toward achieving that goal.

170. C) Because traditional project management activities are distributed among the Scrum roles

Explanation: Scrum distributes the responsibilities traditionally held by a project manager among its three roles: Product Owner, Scrum Master, and Development Team. This decentralized approach allows for more self-organization and empowerment within the team, rendering the role of a traditional project manager unnecessary in the Scrum framework.

171. D) Scrum is a framework that aligns with the Agile Manifesto principles

Explanation: Scrum is a framework that aligns with the principles of the Agile Manifesto, providing a structured approach to agile software development.

172. C) A process that is based on observation, experimentation, and evidence.

Explanation: Empirical process control in Scrum emphasizes making decisions based on real-world observations, experimentation, and feedback rather than relying solely on theoretical or predetermined

Answers

plans. This approach allows for adaptability and continuous improvement based on the actual outcomes and experiences encountered during the project.

173. B) Focus, Courage, Commitment, Openness, and Respect

Explanation: The Scrum values that should be present in a Scrum event, artifact, or role are Focus, Courage, Commitment, Openness, and Respect.

174. C) Because it provides a broad structure under which various processes and techniques can be employed.

Explanation: Scrum is considered a framework rather than a methodology because it provides a broad structure under which various processes and techniques can be employed, allowing for flexibility and adaptation.

175. B) Three roles: the Scrum Master, the Product Owner, and the Development Team.

Explanation: A Scrum Team consists of three roles: the Scrum Master, the Product Owner, and the Development Team, each with specific responsibilities.

176. C) Assigning specific tasks to Development Team members.

Explanation: Assigning specific tasks to Development Team members is not a prerogative of the Product Owner. The Development Team self-organizes and determines how to best accomplish the work.

Answers

177. B) To ensure that there is a clear, singular vision for the product.

Explanation: Having a single Product Owner ensures that there is a clear direction and vision for the product, avoiding conflicting priorities or diluted decision-making that could arise from having a committee. This clarity helps streamline communication and decision-making processes within the Scrum framework, ultimately leading to more effective product development.

178. B) A potentially releasable product increment.

Explanation: At the end of every sprint, the goal is to deliver a potentially releasable product increment, meaning that the work completed during the sprint is in a condition where it could potentially be released to stakeholders or customers if they choose to do so. This incremental delivery approach ensures that value is continuously delivered and allows for regular feedback and adaptation.

179. C) Facilitating the dialogue between the team and the Product Owner.

Explanation: During sprint planning, the Scrum Master's responsibility includes facilitating the discussion between the Development Team and the Product Owner to ensure that the team understands the items in the product backlog and the expectations for the sprint. This helps to clarify any uncertainties and ensure alignment between the team and the Product Owner regarding the sprint goal and the work to be undertaken.

Answers

180. C) The extra development work that arises when code that is easy to implement in the short run is used instead of applying the best overall solution.

Explanation: Technical debt in Scrum refers to the extra development work that arises when code that is easy to implement in the short run is used instead of applying the best overall solution, leading to future complications or rework.

181. C) An iterative, incremental framework for development

Explanation: Scrum is an iterative, incremental framework for managing complex projects, primarily used in software development but applicable to various industries.

182. C) Up to a month

Explanation: The duration of a Sprint in Scrum is typically up to a month, with most Sprints lasting between one to four weeks.

183. C) A cross-functional team selects items to complete

Explanation: At the beginning of a Sprint, a cross-functional team selects items from the product backlog to complete during the Sprint based on the Sprint goal and their capacity.

184. C) A working product that is "done."

Explanation: At the end of a sprint in Scrum, the expected outcome is a working product increment that meets the Definition of Done. This means the product increment is fully functional, potentially

Answers

shippable, and adds value, demonstrating progress towards the overall product goals.

185. A) Inspect and adapt

Explanation: The central theme in Scrum is "inspect and adapt," emphasizing the iterative and incremental nature of the framework, where teams regularly inspect their work and adapt their processes to improve continuously.

186. B) Cross-functional teams empowered to make decisions

Explanation: Agile development focuses on cross-functional teams empowered to make decisions, enabling collaboration and faster delivery of value to customers.

187. C) A restart in the game of rugby

Explanation: The term "Scrum" originates from Rugby, which refers to a method of restarting play after a minor infringement, symbolizing the collaborative and adaptive approach of the Scrum framework.

188. B) The game of Rugby

Explanation: The 1986 Harvard Business Review article related successful development to the game of Rugby, which inspired Jeff Sutherland and Ken Schwaber, the founders of Scrum, to apply its principles to software development.

189. C) Jeff Sutherland and Ken Schwaber

Answers

Explanation: Jeff Sutherland and Ken Schwaber are the founders of Scrum, developing the framework based on empirical process control, iterative development, and collaboration principles.

190. B) To re-plan work to meet commitments

Explanation: Daily meetings during a Sprint, known as the Daily Scrum or Stand-up, are to inspect progress, identify impediments, and re-plan work as necessary to meet commitments.

191. A) A guided missile

Explanation: Scrum is often likened to a guided missile because it can be highly effective when aimed correctly. Like a guided missile, Scrum allows for adjustments and corrections along the way to ensure the team stays on course toward its objectives, adapting to changes and obstacles as they arise.

192. A) Outmoded business practices

Explanation: The Scrum framework helps to transform outmoded business practices by promoting agility, adaptability, and responsiveness to change in complex and uncertain environments.

193. B) A better life and extreme business value

Explanation: Scrum encourages collaboration, transparency, and delivering value to stakeholders, leading to improved outcomes and a better work environment for developers and stakeholders.

Answers

194. C) 1993

Explanation: The first Scrum project was initiated in 1993 when Jeff Sutherland and his team at Easel Corporation applied Scrum principles to software development.

195. D) Ericsson

Explanation: While Google, Amazon, and Microsoft are commonly known for using Scrum, Ericsson has not been mentioned in the context of utilizing Scrum.

196. C) The official guide defining the Scrum framework

Explanation: "The Scrum Guide" is the official guide defining the Scrum framework, providing guidelines and principles for implementing Scrum in organizations.

197. B) Building working software quickly

Explanation: Agile principles' primary focus is building working software quickly, fostering customer collaboration, and responding to change effectively.

198. C) Sprints

Explanation: Scrum structures development into fixed-length iterations called Sprints, typically lasting one to four weeks, during which a potentially shippable product increment is created.

199. B) A collection of Scrum case studies

Answers

Explanation: The Scrum Papers refer to a collection of Scrum case studies that document experiences and insights from organizations implementing Scrum in various contexts.

200. C) Improvements in productivity and morale

Explanation: Teams that effectively implement Scrum often report improvements in both productivity and morale. This is because Scrum promotes better communication, collaboration, and a clear focus on delivering valuable increments of work, which can lead to a more motivated and efficient team.

201. C) They end on a specific date whether work is completed or not

Explanation: Sprints in Scrum have a fixed duration, typically ranging from one to four weeks. They end on a specific date, known as the Sprint end date, regardless of whether all the planned work has been completed. This timeboxed approach promotes predictability and encourages the team to focus on delivering a potentially shippable product increment within the defined timeframe.

202. D) 1993

Explanation: Scrum was formalized into a framework in 1993 by Jeff Sutherland and his team at Easel Corporation, marking the beginning of its application to software development.

203. B) At www.scrum.org

Answers

Explanation: The fully defined Scrum framework can be found at www.scrum.org, where the Scrum Guide, authored by Ken Schwaber and Jeff Sutherland, provides comprehensive guidelines and principles for implementing Scrum.

204. C) To re-plan work to achieve the Sprint's goals

Explanation: The goal of the daily Scrum meeting, also known as the Daily Stand-up, is for the Development Team to synchronize activities, identify any obstacles, and re-plan work as necessary to achieve the Sprint's goals.

205. C) Whenever the team decides

Explanation: Sprints in Scrum are conducted whenever the Scrum Team decides, typically lasting one to four weeks, depending on the project's context and requirements.

206. A) A product ready for release

Explanation: In Scrum, "potentially shippable" refers to a product increment that is complete, fully functional, and meets the Definition of Done. It is in a state where, if the stakeholders choose to do so, it could be released without further work. This approach encourages continuous delivery of value and ensures that each increment of work is of high quality and potentially usable by end-users.

207. C) Ken Schwaber and Jeff Sutherland

Explanation: Ken Schwaber and Jeff Sutherland are the co-creators of Scrum and are responsible for maintaining and evolving the Scrum

Answers

Guide, which serves as the definitive guide to the Scrum framework. They continue to contribute to its development and ensure it remains relevant and effective for Scrum practitioners worldwide.

208. D) A hierarchical structure

Explanation: A Scrum team is encouraged to build a collaborative and self-organizing environment rather than a hierarchical structure, promoting shared responsibility, ownership, and accountability among team members.

209. B) Because it is simple and powerful

Explanation: Scrum is powerful because it is simple and focuses on core principles such as transparency, inspection, and adaptation, enabling teams to respond quickly to change and deliver value iteratively.

210. C) An inspection and adaptation of the product and practices

Explanation: After a development step in Scrum, the framework requires an inspection and adaptation of both the product increment and the team's processes, allowing for continuous improvement and alignment with customer needs.

211. C) Prioritizing the Product Backlog

Explanation: The primary function of the Product Owner in Scrum is to prioritize the Product Backlog, ensuring that the team works on the most valuable items first and maximizing the product's value.

Answers

212. B) 1-4 weeks

Explanation: Sprints in a Scrum project typically last 1-4 weeks, with the duration determined based on factors such as the project's complexity, the team's velocity, and stakeholder expectations.

213. C) To select items from the Product Backlog for the upcoming Sprint

Explanation: The Sprint Planning Meeting in Scrum is held to select items from the Product Backlog that the Development Team will work on during the upcoming Sprint, as well as to establish the Sprint Goal and create a plan for achieving it.

214. C) A set of granulated steps for items selected for the Sprint

Explanation: The Sprint Backlog in Scrum is a set of granulated steps or tasks derived from the Product Backlog items selected for the Sprint, representing the work that the Development Team plans to complete during the Sprint.

215. B) 15 minutes

Explanation: The Daily Stand-Up Meeting in Scrum typically lasts for 15 minutes, providing a brief opportunity for the Development Team to synchronize activities, identify any obstacles, and plan their work for the day.

216. B) Product Owner, Team Members, Scrum Master, and stakeholders

Answers

Explanation: The Sprint Review in Scrum is attended by the Scrum Team (Product Owner, Development Team, Scrum Master) and stakeholders, including customers, users, and anyone else interested in the product's progress.

217.   B) To discuss what's working and what's not

Explanation: The goal of the Sprint Retrospective is to enable the Scrum Team to inspect and adapt their processes, tools, and collaboration methods. It provides an opportunity for the team to reflect on the previous sprint, identify areas of improvement, and make actionable plans for implementing those improvements in the upcoming sprints.

218.   B) Sequential life cycle

Explanation: The Waterfall model follows a sequential approach, where each phase must be completed before the next one begins. It is a linear and non-iterative process.

219.   D) Just before the product launch

 Explanation: In the Waterfall model, creativity is often expected to occur just before the product launch. This is because, in the Waterfall approach, each phase is completed sequentially, with little room for changes or creativity once a phase is finished. Therefore, any adjustments or last-minute changes tend to happen toward the end of the project, typically before the product is ready for launch.

220.   C) They are often not read or are misunderstood

Copyright © 2024 VERSAtile Reads. All rights reserved.
This material is protected by copyright, any infringement will be dealt with legal and punitive action.

Answers

Explanation: A significant drawback of using written documents in the Waterfall approach is that they are often not read or are misunderstood, leading to misalignment and communication issues.

221. D) After the product launch

Explanation: Valuable insights into the product typically emerge in the Waterfall model after the product launch when it is issued by real users in real-world scenarios.

222. C) It assumes humans can predict the future accurately

Explanation: A fundamental problem with the Waterfall model related to planning is that it assumes humans can predict the future accurately, leading to rigid plans that may not accommodate changes.

223. B) It creates an adversarial relationship between team members

Explanation: The Waterfall model tends to create an adversarial relationship between team members due to its sequential nature, which can negatively affect morale and collaboration.

224. B) Mediocre products

Explanation: The result of a rigid, change-resistant process like the Waterfall model tends to be mediocre products that may not fully meet customer needs or expectations.

225. A) To adopt a different model like Scrum

Explanation: A common reaction to the problems experienced with the Waterfall model is to adopt a different model like Scrum, which offers more flexibility and adaptability.

Answers

226.   C) Easel Corporation

Explanation: Easel Corporation was the first company to create a Scrum team.

227.   B) 4 weeks

Explanation: In Scrum, the maximum length of a Sprint is indeed four weeks. This duration provides sufficient time for the team to deliver a valuable increment while still maintaining a sense of adaptability and responsiveness to change. Thank you for pointing out the mistake!

228.   A) Dr. Jeff Sutherland and Ken Schwaber

Explanation: Dr. Jeff Sutherland and Ken Schwaber formalized the Scrum framework in 1995.

229.   D) Sprint Planning Meeting

Explanation: The Sprint Planning Meeting in Scrum focuses on what will be developed in the next Sprint, including selecting items from the Product Backlog and defining the Sprint Goal.

230.   C) The Product Owner

Explanation: In a Scrum project, the Product Owner is responsible for maximizing Return on Investment (ROI) by prioritizing the Product Backlog items based on their value and ensuring that the team delivers the most valuable increments of work in each sprint.

Answers

This involves making strategic decisions about what features or enhancements will bring the most value to the product and its stakeholders.

231. C) Daily Stand-Up Meeting

Explanation: The Daily Stand-Up Meeting, also known as the Daily Scrum, is a key practice that the Scrum Team engages in daily. It is a short, time-box meeting where team members synchronize their activities, discuss progress toward the sprint goal, and identify any impediments or obstacles that need to be addressed. This daily communication helps to keep the team aligned, focused, and responsive to changes.

232. C) The Waterfall

Explanation: Traditional software development, characterized by a sequential, linear approach to project management, is commonly known as the Waterfall model. In this model, phases such as requirements gathering, design, implementation, testing, and maintenance follow a sequential flow, with each phase being completed before the next one begins.

233. B) Inspect and adapt

Explanation: A significant theme in Scrum regarding product development is the iterative and incremental approach of "inspect and adapt." Scrum emphasizes continuous improvement through regular inspection of progress and adaptation of plans based on feedback and changing requirements. This iterative process allows for flexibility, responsiveness to customer needs, and the ability to deliver value incrementally.

Answers

234. D) Fully documented

Explanation: While documentation may be important, it is not always a requirement for something to be considered "done" in Scrum. "Done" typically means that the increment is potentially shippable, meets the Definition of Done, is fully tested, and integrated. Documentation may vary depending on the team's agreement and the nature of the project.

235. B) By a product vision created by the Product Owner

Explanation: Scrum projects are driven by a product vision created by the Product Owner, which guides the development team in delivering value to stakeholders.

236. B) A prioritized list of requirements

Explanation: The Product Backlog in Scrum is a prioritized list of requirements, features, enhancements, and fixes that constitute the changes to be made to the product in future releases.

237. C) The Scrum Master

Explanation: The Scrum Master is responsible for removing impediments that may block the Scrum Team's progress, ensuring that the team can work effectively and efficiently.

238. B) 5-9 people

Answers

Explanation: The recommended size for a Scrum Team is typically 5-9 people, small enough to remain agile and large enough to complete significant work within a Sprint.

239. C) A product or increment that is ready for use at the end of each Sprint

Explanation: In Scrum, "potentially shippable" refers to a product or increment that has been completed to the Definition of Done by the end of the sprint. It means the work is of high quality and in a state where it could potentially be released or deployed if the stakeholders choose to do so. This approach allows for continuous delivery of value and promotes transparency and accountability within the Scrum framework.

240. A) Product Owner, Scrum Master, and Team Members

Explanation: The Scrum team comprises the Product Owner, Scrum Master, and Team Members, who work together to deliver increments of potentially shippable functionality at the end of each Sprint.

241. C) They are time-boxed and fixed in duration.

Explanation: Sprints in Scrum are timeboxed iterations of development work, meaning they have a fixed duration, typically measured in weeks, and they do not extend beyond their predetermined length.

242. C) Requirements are fixed and selected at the beginning of the Sprint.

Answers

Explanation: In Scrum, customer requirements are fixed and selected at the beginning of the Sprint during the Sprint Planning meeting. These requirements remain unchanged throughout the Sprint to maintain focus and stability.

243. C) Code that is integrated, thoroughly tested, and potentially shippable.

Explanation: The primary goal of a Sprint in Scrum is to produce a potentially shippable product increment, which means the code developed during the Sprint is integrated, thoroughly tested, and ready for deployment if needed.

244. C) Inspect and adapt

Explanation: Central to Scrum's philosophy of continuous improvement is the principle of "inspect and adapt." Scrum encourages teams to regularly inspect their processes, products, and progress and to adapt their plans and behaviors accordingly. This iterative approach fosters learning, innovation, and the ability to respond effectively to changing requirements and circumstances throughout the project.

245. C) Empowering cross-functional teams to make decisions

Explanation: The fundamental goal of Agile development methods like Scrum is to empower cross-functional teams to make decisions collaboratively. Agile emphasizes iterative and incremental delivery, frequent customer feedback, and the ability to adapt to changing requirements. This approach fosters collaboration, creativity, and innovation within the team, ultimately leading to the delivery of high-quality products that meet customer needs.

Answers

246. C) Both utilize rapid iteration and continuous input

Explanation: The analogy drawn between Scrum and Rugby highlights their shared emphasis on rapid iteration and continuous input, reflecting the dynamic and adaptive nature of both approaches.

247. C) Professors Takeuchi and Nonaka

Explanation: Professors Takeuchi and Nonaka introduced the term "Scrum" in their 1986 Harvard Business Review article, which likened successful product development to the game of Rugby.

248. B) Scrum has revolutionized product development with its simplicity and effectiveness

Explanation: The text emphasizes Scrum's significant impact on product development, portraying it as a simple yet powerful framework that has led to improvements and transformations in productivity and morale.

249. C) Apple

Explanation: Apple is not mentioned in the list of companies using Scrum provided in the text.

250. B) Delivering extreme business value to customers.

Explanation: The ultimate goal of Scrum is to deliver extreme business value to customers by focusing on building communities of

Answers

stakeholders, improving the lives of developers, and releasing creativity and team spirit in practitioners.

About Our Products

About Our Products

Other products from VERSAtile Reads are:

 Elevate Your Leadership: The 10 Must-Have Skills

 Elevate Your Leadership: 8 Effective Communication Skills

 Elevate Your Leadership: 10 Leadership Styles for Every Situation

 300+ PMP Practice Questions Aligned with PMBOK 7, Agile Methods, and Key Process Groups – 2024

 Exam-Cram Essentials Last-Minute Guide to Ace the PMP Exam - Your Express Guide featuring PMBOK® Guide

 Career Mastery Blueprint - Strategies for Success in Work and Business

 Memory Magic: Unraveling the Secret of Mind Mastery

 The Success Equation Psychological Foundations For Accomplishment

 Fairy Dust Chronicles – The Short and Sweet of Wonder

 B2B Breakthrough – Proven Strategies from Real-World Case Studies

Copyright © 2024 VERSAtile Reads. All rights reserved.
This material is protected by copyright, any infringement will be dealt with legal and punitive action.

About Our Products

 CISSP Fast Track: Master CISSP Essentials for Exam Success

 CISA Fast Track: Master CISA Essentials for Exam Success

 CISM Fast Track: Master CISM Essentials for Exam Success

 CCSP Fast Track: Master CCSP Essentials for Exam Success

www.ingramcontent.com/pod-product-compliance
Lightning Source LLC
Chambersburg PA
CBHW082338220526
45470CB00008B/2558